Praise for *Back to Love Again*

"If you want to make positive, life-enhancing changes to your life, Nicole Thibodeau's book, *Back to Love Again* is a *must-read*. I especially liked 'Love, The Ultimate Tool That Heals from the Inside and Fortifies Us' in Chapter 10."

— Randall Monk, Author/Self-Help/Spiritual Teacher,
   TimelyGuidance.com

"This is a book of great compassion. I have known Nicole for almost twenty years. I am honored to be the first to read her book. She has touched my heart with her sensitivity and the beauty of her life's testimony throughout the pages. It is an intimate journey to return to love, peace, and harmony. I thought it was great that each thematic chapter was completed by a meditation and a Code of Light to accompany us to our own awareness, to our own inner healing of heart and soul.

The strength of her courage and humility encourages each woman to find herself, to take herself in hand, to welcome herself in compassion without judgment, to discover her strengths and qualities, and to love herself enough to enter into her power and transform her life positively.

May you benefit from this book. May it become your bedside or reference book in the cycles of your life and always bring you the grace of transformation and the hope of new days."

— Jacqueline Celestine Joachim, Author, *MaShaBa – La Mère Divine en Soi*

D1554363

"In *Back to Love Again*, Nicole Thibodeau weaves her beautiful story of personal evolution and healing from the humble beginnings of a violent and traumatic childhood, where her closest friends were her Angels, to how she became the Oracle of Divine Transmission, channeling the Divine Mothers, Angels, Archangels, and Ascended Beings. Each chapter is infused with high vibrational meditations and a coded image to activate Divine change and transformation in the reader. Just by looking at the Codes, I can feel Divine energy swirling in my body! It's amazing. I highly recommend this book to sensitive souls who've struggled on their journey to self-love because each chapter is like a mini-healing towards massive transformation!"

— Dr. Karen Kan, founder of the Academy of Light Medicine, and best-selling author of *Sensitivity is Your Superpower*

"This work by Nicole Thibodeau is a work of love and of great courage. She lays bare her trials and tribulations in her self-actualization journey. When reading, one becomes inspired to find solutions to life by journeying inwards. I have witnessed the wonderful work that Nicole is doing through her meditations and unique Codes and sounds and have seen how it heals and gives hope to many seekers. A very inspiring work with transformative meditations and Codes."

— Ma Mokshapriya Shakti, PhD

"Nicole is the real deal. *Back to Love Again* is an initiation and a call from deep inside for you to remember the truth of who you are. It is an inspired mix of divinely co-created artwork, spiritual memoir, and channeled grace. This book will enable you to shift with its vibration alone — and when you apply the information to your life, hang on to your crystals! You are in for quite a ride on the wings of unconditional Love straight into the realms of self-mastery."

— Theresa Vee, Intuitive Guide and Transformation Teacher

Back to Love Again

A Giver's Guide to Reconnect with Your Inner Strength

NICOLE THIBODEAU

 Published by: Capucia, LLC
211 Pauline Drive #513
York, PA 17402

Paperback ISBN: 978-1-954920-26-2
eBook ISBN: 978-1-954920-27-9
Library of Congress Control Number: 2022908626

Cover Design: Ranilo Cabo
Layout: Ranilo Cabo
Photographer: Rose aux joues Photographie & Coaching/www.roseauxjoues.com
Book Midwife: Carrie Jareed

Printed in the United States of America

To you beautiful hearts that are feeling overwhelmed, overworked, or lost on your journey and yet you still seek peace in your heart. It is possible to be at peace within through self-love. This book is a gift from my heart to yours.

Contents

Foreword

Dear Friends,

Most people have no idea what is involved in becoming a Cosmic Telepath, or a person who agrees to bring forth inspired information/ teachings from the higher realms of existence. First, before we incarnated in this lifetime, we made an agreement to become a messenger of the solar system, galactic, and even possibly, Universal information. Especially over the last forty years or so, we have been blessed with step-by-step teachings, tools, methods, and meditations to assist us to move through the many levels and vibrational planes of awareness, which will eventually lead to Self-awareness and Self-Mastery.

We have learned that we are not alone, and we never have been. And amazingly, we have learned about and are experiencing our miraculous connections to our Guardian Angels, Celestial Teachers, Guides, and our Soul Family. We have learned how we were separated for eons of time so that we could fulfill and experience our many Divine missions, and so we could gain the expertise we needed to become co-creative Self-Masters. That is what Nicole Thibodeau shares in her heartwarming story and the loving transmissions from Divine Mother and other Beings of Light.

To assume such a cosmic assignment, such as Nicole and so many other dedicated Souls like me have accepted, it must become a major priority and a life-time endeavor. First, it takes a burning desire to fulfill your spiritual mission and a willingness to gain all the knowledge, expertise, and qualities it takes to become a speaker/teacher and conveyer of knowledge. It is sometimes a lonely journey, and you must learn to accept rejection, criticism, and judgment graciously and not allow it to deter you from your chosen path. Without being aware of it, most often many of the trials, tests, and experiences throughout your lifetime are designed to prepare you for your ultimate profession as a conveyer of godly wisdom.

It is not an easy task to share our painful experiences, and it takes great tenacity, dedication, and courage to write a book such as this. However, by sharing our personal stories, the painful experiences, the sometimes mind-boggling and confusing transition process, and the many miracles along the way, our hope is that it will make your "Rite of Passage into Self-Mastery" a little easier.

If you are looking for a Fast Track to Wholeness in preparation for Self-Mastery, which is a critical component of the Ascension Process, then *Back to Love Again* is the book for you. Eternal love and Angel Blessings to all my dear Soul companions on the journey,

Ronna Vezane
Author, Lecturer, and Spiritual Counselor
StarQuestMastery.com

Introduction

It is amazing how life can take a sudden turn, and you find yourself at the stage where you need to reinvent yourself. So many events occur in your life which make you doubt yourself, deny yourself, and yet you feel this need, this urgency, to bring changes from within. You feel your heart, your soul nudging you; you have an inexplicable *knowing* that it is time for you to come Back to Love Again.

Even if you have lost your way to yourself or you feel overwhelmed, knowing that it is possible, through self-love, to redefine yourself, you can rediscover and reconnect to the loving self within you and your Divine Power. It is possible for you to feel the freedom that loving thyself brings by breaking the inner chains of what is holding you back in your life. Also, to know that all the changes you go through from within can happen with grace, harmony, and in complete gentleness.

My life had many twists and turns for me to overcome before I was finally able to come back to self-love. I say *Back to Love Again* because we are all born connected to this love as we *are* love. Only, as time goes by, we sometimes lose our deep connection to our divine essence, Love. Growing up in a dysfunctional family, living through my parents' ugly divorce, and with unresolved grief throughout the years as well as the denial of my inner gifts, I lost myself and ended up in burnout, which brought me on my spiritual path back to self-love. Of course, there were ups and downs, but with determination and my heart's longing to be in the love-energy, I began a very special journey. Like the Phoenix that rose from the ashes, I dove deeply into the depths of my being, reconnecting to my Divine Presence through meditations and energy healing sessions. With the embrace and support of my Divine Team, I learned to connect to love as a way to heal myself from within and come to a place of self-love and a peaceful heart.

The title *Back to Love Again* came to me first. Then one day, I was guided by Divine Mother to write this book, which holds many channeled meditations and sacred Codes (frequency-infused images).

As you hold this book in your hands, you know you have been guided to this book for a reason. You will receive Divine Mother's love through your entire being as you hold and read this book. The meditations and Codes become your tool kit to use as needed in your life. Divine Mother will hold you in her loving embrace for you to feel safe and supported so you can move through the clearings, liberations and healings on your journey with ease and grace. You will be brought on your own journey back to the love of your sacred heart.

May this book touch the hearts of all those who are meant to be the love-sowers, the bearers of the Divine Truth, of Divine Love and ignite the spark within them and let them know they are not alone, and it is time to come *Back to Love Again*. May our world have more peace as you discover the freedom that love can bring within you and to those around you. As a wave of love spreads to all past generations to heal, to one's family heart, one's lineage's heart, community, and the world. Each person reading this book brings his/her own color of love to the world.

May this book help people to connect to love again deeply and truly and to stop fearing the love that we all hold within. For all to be empowered and know they are Love.

Love and blessings,
Nicole Thibodeau

Author's Note

In each chapter, you have a guided meditation. For utmost success, I suggest you download the free Divine Connection Booster through this link: *https://bit.ly/ConnectionBooster*. Your Divine Connection will ground your energies deeply into the Earth and connect you to Source. You will be connecting to the 7th Dimension or higher where there is no duality, only unity. This is particularly important for you to do prior to doing the meditations and when activating the Codes of Light (high-frequency, encoded images).

The mantras with the Codes are in *light language*. Some vowels are pronounced a certain way for example:

A as in apple

E as ay in say

I as ee in see

O is standard long o sound as in go

U as oo in smooth

Y as in eye.

Enjoy singing these mantras in long resonant tones.

CHAPTER 1

The Valley of Fear

Growing Up in Fear

Living in fear is never easy, and unfortunately for some of us this is learned at a very young age. Obviously, no one should ever have to live this way, always having to watch your back. It is exhausting to keep a constant watch on your behavior, so you don't upset your parents or because you fear creating a new crisis in the home. As a child, the shouting, name calling, and screaming scared me a lot, but the beatings left undisputedly deep emotional scars. When this would happen, I would stand still, barely breathing. It even felt at times as if I was stepping out of my body. I did not want to be there living in this fear, so much so that at five years old I wanted out. I asked God to take me back home because I could not survive in this. It was way too difficult, and I could not feel love. At that moment I saw a vision that there would be a loving, caring man who would come into my life someday and I would be happy. This first vision of my future gave me hope.

Nonetheless, I became so fearful of everyone and everything that I was extra careful in all I was doing. Hypervigilance became my second nature, and my saviour too. It saved me from arguments that would aggravate into hurtful situations. I was always very nice, trying to please all and make sure everyone was happy and felt supported. But there is only so much you can do when you are five, six, seven, eight or nine-years-old. I carried this fear into my teenage years and even until my mid-thirties, where this desire to please others turned me into a perfectionist. This behaviour served others and pleased me also until I started to feel unhappy, or I felt people were demanding too much from me.

I was ten years-old when my parents divorced. The process was atrocious. My sister Lise, who is twelve years older than I am, had been married for three years already at that time. It was so horrible that we left the house while my father was away. When my father realised we were gone, he went into such a rage. We hid at my sister Lise's house, keeping low so he wouldn't see us in the house. We could hear him shouting outside, screaming and calling my mom all kinds of names. During that time my sister Lucie, who is almost three years older than I, were holding each other so tight, because we were so frightened. Lucie was trying to protect me. She was thirteen; I was ten.

Shortly after that, my mother decided to send us to an uncle's house for a few weeks to hide and make sure nothing would happen to us. When we came back a few weeks later, we had an apartment to live in and my mom was waiting for my dad to deliver the furniture to us. We lived on the second floor, and I was sitting outside on the steps of the long, curvy staircase. When my dad arrived, he was enraged and broke all the furniture in front of us, claiming that if he couldn't have it, neither could we. I still remember the sadness I felt inside as my heart sank to the bottom of my body, thinking to myself that it was so sad that my dad wasn't thinking of me or my needs. I didn't count in this equation. It was pathetic.

Summer ended and it was time to start school. I was going to a new school. I didn't know what to think of this. I was really uneasy with it, but I was raised to face the hard times head-on, so I went. I was different from the other children as we were part of the first wave of kids from divorced parents. Because of this we were the talk of the town. Everyone at school would look at me as if I had a bad disease or as if I was an alien. Remember that in the early '70s, religion was still going strong; therefore, children of divorced parents were bad people, and their parents were excluded from church. It was a sin to divorce. Plus, back then, if women left their husbands, they were not entitled to have guardianship of their children. In 1968 in the Province of Quebec, women could file for divorce, but it was only in July 1972 that women were allowed to have guardianship of their children if they left. It was only in 1977 that rights became equal for a woman, when it came to the guardianship of her children, when she left the house and filed for divorce. Before that, only the father had the power of authority. It was called the *power of paternity*.

Because of those laws, my mother waited to file for divorce until the law passed in 1972 so she could fight for our guardianship, as she did not want to leave us with our dad because she feared something harmful could happen to us. Because of all these old laws, people, unaware of the new laws, would look at us in complete judgment and disgrace. In my former school, I was judged because of my father and teased about it; they were pointing at me and whispering as I went by because my parents were divorced. Nothing could have prepared me for these hurtful moments. I felt isolated and had no one to talk to or confide in and felt deeply hurt and misunderstood. Little did I know that that was only the beginning of a very difficult and hard year.

My dad's harassment sent my mother into such a very deep depression that she was hospitalized. Because my mother was in the hospital and she was our legal guardian, it was decided by the youth protection agency that my sister Lucie and I would be sent to a foster home, not my dad's, because of all the complaints already filed against him. So, legally, it was out of the question for us to live with my dad. I cried myself to sleep that first night in my sister Lucie's arms. I had just turned eleven and she was fourteen. Sometime later, I was sent to my older brother Yvon's house as he was married and fifteen years my elder. Lucie stayed at the foster home as this woman could only keep one of us. It was decided that my brother was to be my foster home from now on. The drive there was an agony—two hours without a word from the social worker. So many questions were going through my mind at that time, but I was so intimidated by this woman that I did not dare speak, especially since she had seated me in the back. I wanted to cry, but I didn't dare. I had to be brave even if I did not understand anything about what was really going on. I wanted to stay with my mother. My thoughts raced. *Why couldn't I stay with my mom? Why wasn't Lucie coming with me? Will I come back?* They told me that it was temporary until my mom could move to Montreal, and that was the end of it. No other questions were to be asked, and the matter was not open for discussion. This emotional two-hour drive was the longest ever in my young life.

I changed schools again. I had to adapt. The good thing was my brother had a ten-month-old baby girl, and I was longing to love someone. Receiving her unconditional love back was a blessing for my soul. But then my brother moved, so I had to change schools again. I got to a point where I thought, *Why bother trying to make friends?* and withdrew within myself. The kids were nice to me, but I thought, *It's no use to make new friends if I'm going to lose them.*

Then the unimaginable happened; my mother had a car accident and almost died. I was eleven at the time and so afraid. I was afraid to lose my mother, the only kind person I trusted, afraid of the way my brother was driving to get to the hospital, afraid of the unknown future coming my way. What would happen to us, her children? We made it, safe and sound, to the hospital under the usual amount of time needed to drive there. Even with all that fear, I was longing to see my mom. *I want to see Mom,* I cried repeatedly. When my sister Alice, (who is nine years older than me) noticed the nurses weren't looking, she snuck me in to see my mom. I loved her for doing this, despite knowing that it was prohibited for me at eleven years old to enter the intensive care unit.

You can imagine how struck I was when I set eyes on my mother. She was not responsive and had so many tubes attached to her. She seemed dead at first sight. Unsure, I gathered all the courage I had to tell her how much we needed her with us and admitted for the first time that I did not wish to live with my dad. This is when my mother started to react and fight for her life. She was in the hospital for some months, so I stayed with my brother a few months more until the day she left the hospital and moved into a new apartment. The time had come for me to come back home to my mother. Again, I was afraid of the coming future and was devastated to leave my niece, whom I felt so connected to. And, you guessed it, there was a new school again. In that year, I went to four different schools. I managed to end that school year with good marks, and I achieved them because the teacher I had was very caring and encouraging.

After a few weeks in that school, we were playing during recreation when I fell and partially ripped a ligament in my knee. The school principal brought me to the hospital where they put a bandage on my knee. I was to walk the least amount possible and keep my leg up. A few days later I was back in school. Walking to school was difficult, especially walking up the hill. Then a few days after my return to school, one of the kids that lived close to my dad had a message for me from my dad. He said, *One day your dad will be waiting for you after school to pick you up and kidnap you.* I panicked. My dad had done this before, taking me away, and I did not want that to happen again. Plus the fact that I could not walk very fast with my injured knee meant I could forget about running away from him. I think all the students in class could read the fear on my face, as they all decided to walk me home. They said, *You will stand in the middle, and we will stand all around you and no one will be able to take you.* No other children had ever done so much for me before. I felt protected even if I was scared to bits.

As soon as I got home, I told my mother about the message from the student. I did not want that to happen again. The year before, after their separation, my dad had hidden me for a week at his aunts' house after I had a dispute with my sister Lucie, and I ran to him to be safe as my mother wasn't home that night. Instead of providing safety, he kidnapped me and hid me! My great-aunts were very kind, but as a child I thought they were very old. After this event, in my childhood innocence, I never realized that the police car that I kept seeing around me was actually following me around to protect me from being kidnapped again.

When the judge pronounced the divorce final, he ordered my mother to move to the city she was born in, Montreal, if she wanted peace of mind and to avoid any further confrontations with my dad. That was before she had the accident. It was time for yet another move. Once more, we moved, but the school year was over, and I was going to start high school in the fall. As it was, I would have changed schools just the same since I was finishing elementary school and going to high school. I was prepared, as I knew very well how it felt to change schools and have to make new friends again. I believed life was going to be better because my mother, my sister Lucie, and I were going to live together in Montreal, but not with my older siblings as they were already adults.

A few years passed. My mother had a boyfriend who was an alcoholic. He was quiet as a mouse when he was drunk. He would sleep off the booze he drank. One time he was drunk for more than a week, and I became apprehensive, so one night I slept at a friend's house to stay away from this situation. Eventually my mother and he worked it out, he became sober, and they got married. He was a nice man, but an alcoholic still, and one day he started to drink again. At that time, I was eighteen and had just begun working after finishing my school degree. I had enough of living with him so, I decided to move out. Although my mother was disappointed to see me go, she understood why I wanted to move out, and she helped me buy what I needed for my apartment, but my stepfather wouldn't. He was mad at me for leaving.

Support, What Support?

I took some time to get to know myself as I lived alone. Even at work, a co-worker was harassing me, judging me because my parents were divorced, until one day I had enough. I was mean with my words, and I didn't like having to confront him, but it was a question of survival to me. I wouldn't allow him or anyone else to bring me down.

I started reading books that would give me tools to work with, to help me open up to my true self. I had learned to walk through the valley of fear; surely I could learn how to work with fear. I could either tame it or face it. Anything I had not learned as a child, I had to learn now. Back then, there was no counselling and not much emotional support for you because your parents were divorced. Even the psychologists didn't know much about these situations and their impact on the family, the parents, or the children. It was a time when you just had to roll up your sleeves, pull up your pants, and move forward, and don't forget to keep your chin up!

Those were the rules to survive: *Forget about it all and move on.* Well, for myself I hid some of it deeply within or carried it as a heavy backpack until I was tired enough and chose to change things. It took me a while to realize that.

The Crossing

Living in stressful situations, such as always making sure all was perfect for my parents so I wouldn't upset them, or hiding when my dad came home drunk, or when I feared for my life while my father was beating my mother up, was no easy thing. I had to be very brave to go through these events. To make it through, I always turned to the heavens, to God, to Mother Mary, and the Angels. As far as I can remember, I always talked to them as if they were standing there right beside me, just like I spoke to my friends. Many times they were my *only* friends, so I was very direct with them, such as asking them, *Why did you leave me here all alone?* Or I would try to say a prayer, and when I couldn't remember the words exactly, I told them, *Well, you know what I mean.* I never questioned their presence or their help. I just knew they were there for me. They helped me and supported me to have the courage to stand up for myself and be brave until each of life's storms were over.

The Fear of Being Seen

Despite the insight I gained from books and the work I did on myself, some of the fears remained, like the fear of being seen, being noticed by others, or being judged. To be seen for who I am with my gifts and my talents would mean exposing myself, and that was way too uncomfortable. It was so frightening that sometimes when I had success, I would sabotage myself not to go forward if an opportunity arose for me to share my gifts, or I would even refuse to go ahead and move to a new position or accept a new promotion. I had learned not to make mistakes, and moving up in the corporate ladder meant I could make mistakes. That would mean a huge fall, and my life would crumble down. Or so I thought.

Taming Fear

At some point, I had to change the way I was thinking because this fear was eating away at my health and my joy. I started to notice more and more what happened when I was afraid, why I was afraid, and what it triggered in me. Taming the fear was no easy task; it was like having the biggest, scariest beast in front of you. I asked myself what tools did I have that would help me to stand in front of my fear and face it exactly the way I was brought up, standing up in adversity? Yes, I found a way to put my fear to good use. I changed my perception of fear and chose to use it to not only serve me, but to save me. Meditation helped me a lot too. Talking with the Angels and the Divine was always something I did, so I kept asking to be guided to what was the best for me.

So, little by little, I started to face my fears and also to recognize them. One at a time, I would live through a fear by acknowledging *it is there* and breathing into it to release it as much as I could. The *out-breath* was the liberation and then later on I added *breathing in love, exhaling fear.* This brought me further on my quest of learning how to live through fear. I started to love the fear and welcome it, and each time I faced it and released it, the fear would diminish and have less and less power over me.

Living It

Giving space to the fear *to be* instead of repressing it was quite a different way of being. Truthfully? I was afraid of my fears. So first, I had to learn to feel secure as the fears came up or showed up and trust that I was held and loved by God(dess), and with that, build my self-confidence. From there, I was able to start giving fear *permission to be there* and started tuning in to it; receiving my inner knowledge about it helped me know more about myself and why I was afraid. What was important was to not judge what was there, nor my feelings. I just needed to acknowledge my fear, *and let it be, allow it to exist,* so it could teach me.

This made the process much easier; to be able to acknowledge the fears and to *live with it* for a moment, just the time it takes to recognize it, gave me the space I needed to process it. At times it is a split second; other times it is a few seconds. Nonetheless *it was there*, and I was consciously living with it, acknowledging it, instead of running away from it or burying it deep within my soul.

Loving It and Welcoming It

Once I had acknowledged my fear, I would welcome it, invite it to tell me its story, ask why it was there and did it really belong to me? The easiest way for me to process this is always through breathing. The breath helps keep me centred in my heart and lets me open to let love overflow in my heart. This brings calmness within my being, and I can begin to *send love to that fear* and embrace it. These are the moments when we're fully into our power and great changes or shifts can occur.

Embracing It: Exercises of Connection to Inner Fears

At some point, I started doing some exercises to connect to the fears within me. At first it was just to connect to the fears that I knew were deeply woven in my body and inner self. And, because I was doing this while I was not experiencing the fear in that particular moment, it made the process much easier. I'm not one of those people who intentionally wants to go into past life stories to see if something is there, but rather one who allows *what is there to show up as it is*, wherever it comes from. By being open to what comes, not trying to control it, but rather allowing it to be there and breathe into it, I started having dialogue with some of those fears. These steps were simple, yet very effective. It helped clear the old fears that no longer served me and/or even blocked me from moving forward.

Fear As a Perception Tool

Fear is not only a response to a fight-or-flight situation; it can also become a perception tool. Let me explain. If we take fear as a set of vision glasses which we wear on a daily basis, we will see life situations through these glasses; therefore, all interpretations of situations will be tinted by this fear. However, by healing or releasing this fear, it can no longer affect our vision of life. We have removed the emotional vision glasses that distorted our view and can begin to see the truth.

I started working with the fear, using it as a tool I call a *perception* tool. If we listen carefully, fear helps us to know exactly what is going on within us. Yes, I use it as such because it helps me to see where certain emotions come from or what my next step is. Rather than just reacting based on what my fear is, I give it a chance to teach me. It takes a lot of courage to do this and self-confidence, but we're so worth it because we are the love and light that we seek all the time.

I have let go of those distorted glasses a lot, and I am still doing it as life goes on. New things arise, but it's much simpler to deal with it now since I use fear as a perception tool. Of course, I had to practise to get to this point where I can now embrace the fear and welcome it when it arises in me. It's the perfect indicator of how I feel and where I'm at—in certain situations or in my life progress—in my evolution.

Dialogue With Parts of Us That Hold Fear

With all the channeling and healing sessions I have done, I have witnessed fear showing up as images and even beings, parts of us that once were, perhaps in this lifetime, a past life, a parallel life, or any other lifetime in the universe. Often these parts of us are the ones holding that fear or wound, and they can be triggered by events or situations in our life, and it can awaken that fear in us even though the current situation may not match the fear we feel. All they are trying to do is to protect us, desperately trying to help us avoid going through the ordeal they went through. So, while in a meditative state and assisted by my Angelic team, I was guided to connect through my heart to one fear.

Once connected to it, it was time to send love to this part of me, to who I was in another life, to hold the fear until it felt safe. Then, with an open heart, I started a dialogue with this hidden part of me, receiving its story without judgment. It was very interesting at first because these other life stories don't always make so much sense in the moment, but later on, they do. I learned to be patient with them. The deeper the wound or fear, the more time and love were required for that aspect, that part of me, to heal. During these dialogues, I hold a place of non-judgment, unconditional love, and healing for all involved in the story.

Meditation

Releasing Fear

Through Compassion

When you live in fear or experience many events that create fear in you, you can become what is called *having a hyper-vigilant nature;*

you are always on the lookout to avoid conflicts or attacks. There are many types and various degrees of fear. For now, we will work with the smaller fears as they are easier to work with when alone or working simply with a guided meditation. Begin with the smaller fears, and as it becomes easier to work with them and clear them, you can move on to medium ones. The more you clear the fears, the more space you will have within you to be filled with love and light.

This practice is in three parts. You can do only the guided meditation if you wish for the first time. If you have done this type of work before and feel at ease, you can continue with the exercise that will assist you to connect to your inner fears and release even more. Then, when these two first parts are done, you can do the dialogue. This dialogue will assist you to connect deeply to parts of you that hold fears.

Archangel Raphael will be guiding you through this process along with the Angelic Mothers and Divine Mother.

Step 1: Bringing peace to the parts of you that hold fear.

Beloved one, we are Archangel Raphael. And we invite you now to connect to your heart centre; to feel the energy of love that resides in your heart and ground it to the Earth's core. Receive from the Earth a very soft energy of love and comfort that assists you to stay calm and receive peaceful energies. Also, bring your heart's energies up to Source, igniting each chakra with the love from your heart. In return, Source pours through a beautiful ray of love and peace to support your mind, body, and spirit.

Continue breathing for a moment, allowing the energy of your heart to expand. And now, activate the Emerald Ray through your heart and be with it for a little while. Allow this emerald energy to overflow into all your chakras and all your bodies. Continue to breathe into it. You receive all the support that you need at this moment and time from the Angelic Mothers and Divine Mother, and many more Angelic Beings are coming forth to assist you.

Also, all parts of you who hold fears are now invited in a circle into a temple of healing, where they will receive all the attention needed to assist them in opening up to the process of receiving love and peace so they can be entirely freed from the fears they have been carrying for a long time. These parts of you hold old stories that can bring up fear in you in different situations or any moment in your life. We are bringing different tools for you to work with at this time.

First you need to open your heart to the love flow from all the Angelic Beings gathered around you at this time; they are here to assist you and all these parts of you. Bring your attention to your heart centre and connect to the Emerald Flame that has been activated by your own intention. This Emerald Flame, along with the Flame of Love from your heart—send them now to the heart of those parts of you that need it, letting them know that you are there for them. Reassure them that your intention is pure and that you are ready to invite them to receive the peace energy from Divine Mother, the energy of compassion from the Angelic Mothers and healing energy from the Emerald Ray.

As you breathe gently and profoundly, the more your heart expands in this energy of love, which you can emanate with more ease into their hearts now. With each breath, they receive more love and light, and it brings more and more peace in their hearts too. This assists them to receive more and for the peace to come into their hearts. Continue transmitting into their hearts as long as you feel they are ready to accept to release their fears.

Give thanks to these parts of you that came forward this day to receive from you and to allow this shift to occur within their hearts and your heart.

We love you and bless you.

Archangel Raphael

Note: You can repeat this meditation as often as you wish until you know these aspects and you are ready to move to the next part of this process.

Step 2: Exercise to connect to inner fears (with Code)

As you are sitting in meditation with all the parts of you that hold fear and came to the Divine Mother's temple to receive healing, we invite you to intend from your heart to connect to the fear that is most important for you to connect to. Allow all parts of you to have time to connect to this fear; give them the space to open up to this process by simply breathing deeply and sending love to them. As they receive the love-energy, they become aware that they are well-supported and held and safe.

You are assisted by the Angelic Mothers at this point, who hold you and all aspects of you that hold fear in safety. They sing to them, which helps them to release and to let go of the resistance to opening up and releasing their fears. They are being held by the Angelic Mothers and their teams of Angels in a sacred circle with a beautiful flame of love in the centre mixed with the violet flame.

Imagine yourself standing with them in this circle receiving love from the Angelic Mothers, and with their support, you now connect your heart to the flame in the centre, the flame of love and violet. This connection to these flames is a simple way of connecting to the fears within you and an easy way to release them into the flames.

Once this deep connection is done, intend for all the fears that no longer serve you to be released with ease and grace into these flames. Meanwhile the Angelic Mothers pour elixirs of love and healing into your heart and the heart of all parts of you. These elixirs help to untie old fears that are deeply rooted within you and parts of you. Continue breathing, giving time for the elixirs to pour now through all your chakras. Continue breathing, three more breaths now. And now the elixirs are pouring through all your bodies, particularly your physical body, your emotional body, and your mental body. They all receive these energies and begin to free themselves with more ease and grace.

Again, your breath is key here in releasing the old fears. Now the Angelic Mothers release all ties connected to you and those old fears, all ramifications, all old energies connected to these fears. And as this is being done, you begin to feel more and more liberated and to feel lighter and more peaceful.

You can now take the Code that was drawn for this exercise, which will help to clear even deeper fears, some that are crystallized. This Code is a *Wheel of Compassion*. This Code serves two purposes at the same time. It clears old fears and activates the strength and peace within you so you may have more clarity and be more peaceful within.

Look into this Code. Allow it to come through your third eye chakra, penetrating it, and then it will begin to spin in your third eye. As the wheel begins to spin in your third eye, begin to sing the mantra of it. You will sing it twenty-two times (22X) as the wheel moves through the crown chakra, the soul star chakra. As you continue singing the mantra, the wheel spins into the throat chakra now, going into the heart chakra now. Continue breathing gently as you sing, and the wheel continues to go down into the solar plexus, then the *hara* at the navel level, then into the sacral.

*This Code serves two purposes
at the same time. It clears old fears
and activates the strength and peace
within you so you may have more clarity
and be more peaceful within.*

Continue singing and breathing, and the wheel moves down now into the base chakra, clearing the fears and activating the strength and peace and going down now into the link chakra between your knees, and down now into the Earth Star chakra beneath your feet. Continue singing until you have sung it twenty-two times (22X). Take three deep breaths to anchor the new energies of strength and peace within each chakra and expanding them into your auric field, and allow these energies to flow down into the Earth's heart chakra, grounding deeply these energies into the Earth for you to feel safe, stronger, and more peaceful.

You can use this Code as often as needed, always making sure you connect deeply to all parts of you that hold fear so they, too, can release these fears.

We love you and bless you.

The Angelic Mothers

Step 3: Dialogue with parts of you that hold fear

Once you have deeply connected to the parts of you that hold fear, have sent them love, and have activated the wheel of compassion, you can do this process again to allow some more of them to share with you. Knowing about their fear is not the goal here; it is to discover the gifts they hold for you, the golden nuggets behind the fear that has been released. There is no need to go into the details of the fear; simply receive what this part of you wishes to share and the gift it has for you. It is important that you work with one aspect of yourself at a time in this process.

From the meditation of this chapter:

Bring your attention to your heart centre, breathe deeply, and continue to expand your heart. Invite the part of you that holds the gift that is the highest potential for you in your life at this time to come forth.

Keep breathing deeply. Connect your heart to his or her heart and send more love. The love-energy is key in this exercise. Allow this part of you to speak its truth without judgment nor attachment to what happened to them. All this part of you needs from you at this time is your support and love to help them to clear the blocks that were created by the fear. Your Divine Presence and two guiding Angels who are standing on each side of you are there to assist you through this process.

Continue sending love throughout the process. Take the time that is needed to create the space of trust with your aspect. Once you feel the fear and blocks have been cleared, receive from this aspect the gift that he or she holds for you. Open your heart and receive and give thanks for what you have received.

Give thanks for this aspect having the courage to come forth and share with you. As you are both freed from this process, the gift of love is also enhanced by sharing it. This part of you is coming home to the one heart of your Divine Presence.

Give thanks to these two beautiful Angels that assisted you and to your Divine Presence for oversouling this process.

You are blessed beyond your imagination.
The Angelic Mothers

THE WHEEL OF COMPASSION

Wheel to clear fears and activate Strength, Love, and Peace with the Angelic Mothers.

Nicole Kishalah 2020

OM MARI NAMA 3X OM MA HA (22X)

CHAPTER 2

The River of Emotions

Throughout the years of reading, my favourite books were always spiritual ones, and by doing different types of therapies—mostly alternative ones—I have learned to work with my emotions and make them my friends rather than my enemies. Sailing on the River of Emotions can be tricky at times, other times frightening, or it can be very smooth.

The Crossing

Emotions usually come and go, but sometimes they stick around even when they're uninvited. I know it sounds silly to say, but some days I felt as if I didn't have time for emotions. I was too busy for emotions, forget the ones that linger and just stick to you for days or more. I have always been highly sensitive, and I thought that it was just because I was more touched by events than others. I was criticized because of it, even laughed at, and in elementary school they called me names; that is not counting the fact that at home we were not to show too much emotion.

Emotions had to be refrained and subdued, even the happy ones. So early on, I learned to keep my emotions hidden deeply inside of me because anywhere I went, life was proving to me it was not safe to show your emotions. That was the beginning of what would bring me on a journey of learning how to deal with my emotions—a long one I must admit—but all worth it.

Emotions are like a river; sometimes they flow quietly, other times abundantly, and it can be in between. My first lesson was to accept the emotions as they came. If I were to describe the word emotion, I would say E stands for energy, meaning *E-motion* is energy in motion. Realizing that helped me de-dramatize the fact that I had so many *Energies-in-motion*. If emotions are like a river and I'm the boat, some days I felt like a raft on white waters of the highest category, hanging on tightly so as not to be thrown out and drown. On those days, my world was being rocked to the maximum.

How to Recognize E-Motions?

One day, during a wonderful course that was helping me to land back on my feet and learn what I hadn't learned as a child about my wellbeing, the teacher said, "There are no bad or good emotions, only comfortable or uncomfortable emotions." That made sense to me—recognizing the emotions simply by identifying them as comfortable or not. Ha! Simple enough for me, I thought, but nonetheless it took a weight off my shoulders, or I should say my heart. If I had known that many years ago, it would have de-dramatized and diffused a lot of stress in me.

I began to identify my emotions that way and noticed less panic was showing up about them. I stopped judging myself according to my emotions. If I felt sad, it may have not felt good, but it was okay to feel sad. I wasn't a bad person for feeling sad or angry or disappointed or even joyful when others did not feel joyful. I wasn't laughing at them; I just had this happiness rising in me, and it made me feel good.

Of course, I had a long road ahead of me to integrate this in my life, as old patterns don't go away that easily sometimes. Especially when the old emotions arise, such as the sadness of being laughed at or the fear that I felt when I saw my mother sitting on the floor after my dad had pushed her and she hit her head on the stove. The betrayal I felt when my dad kidnapped me. The shame I felt to be my father's daughter because he was a drunk and violent man. Feeling watched and scrutinized by my father with every move I made. The hurtful names I have been called. Even the teasing from my siblings made me feel inadequate. The anger of being compared to my sister who had died the year before I was born. All the unresolved emotions were there, ready to be embraced and faced. There were many different emotions, and I had to work with them individually.

Facing Your E-Motions

I discovered different techniques to clear emotions. I began with *rebirth*, which is an accompanied breathing technique. This was a good one as it lifted the overflow of emotions I had been repressing all my life. As the overflow of smaller emotions cleared, it gave space for the deeper stored emotions to come to the surface to be resolved. I liked this technique especially because I didn't want to talk to anyone, nor did I want anyone tell me what to do or not to do.

I was angry at life because nothing was working the way I wanted it to. I was wondering, *Why on Earth can't my life be easy like others? Why am I so sensitive to everything in life and to all in my life?* Because of the emotional pain I was feeling inside, I started to push people away: my friends, my family, even my husband. I was hurting so much inside that even the smallest thing like a common insult became a mountain. There was no space left in me to hold any type of emotion.

Once I had done a series of those techniques, and the overflow of emotions was released, I was feeling much better and ready to face my repressed emotions instead of avoiding them or ignoring them. I was ready to sit down with myself and look deeply into my soul and see what was going on. New books were coming out that gave me the guidance I needed. (*Let There be Light* by Ronna Vezane and Archangel Michael). This book had not only messages but recipes in it, the "how to" I desperately needed. I still have that book to this day, and boy does it have many page markers and highlighted sentences! This book gave me the confidence to face up to and live through my emotions and as a result, live a little more.

The Impact on Our Health

Having held back so many emotions, some that were so deeply tucked away from a very young age, started to impact my health and thus my life. Of course, these repressed emotions caused more discomfort in my body: headaches, nausea, irritation of the colon, difficult menstruations (very painful ones), colds, flu and many others. I'm lucky it didn't get worse than that.

Emotions can affect our physical body as well as our mind. I knew it; this had been repeated to me several times. Even my father told me one day, *Girl, you have to accept that you have special gifts. Now you don't have to do anything with them, but you have to accept them, otherwise you will make yourself sick simply by denying them* (meaning who I truly am). This had a huge impact on me. It took years to fully understand the extent of what he had said. So now, when I ignore or refuse something that is so natural for me, I'm automatically redirected to that phrase which switches on a little light in my brain. It says: *Warning, warning, potential threat to your health if you don't deal with this soon!*

Letting Out the Excess of Emotions

Learning how to deal with my emotional state on a daily basis didn't always have the best outcome. Sometimes it came out when I would say things in a wrong way, or I would shout my response because I felt annoyed that people did not *get* me. I didn't mean to hurt anyone. Other times, alone in the house, I would let out a short scream of despair because of the amount of frustration I was not able to let go of. I have tried screaming into a pillow, scribbling the anger out on a piece of paper, writing all that wanted to come out without censoring it nor reading it over so I wouldn't reconnect with it, exercising, and many other things. After all, I owed it to myself to try and see if it worked for me or not, and by doing so, I did learn a little more about myself in that process.

The most important understanding was that the sooner I took care of my emotions, the less of a roller coaster life felt like.

The Tools That Help Keep Us Afloat and Even Overcome the Waves

There are many people out there showing us how to deal with our emotions, but the most important thing is, it must feel true in our hearts. If it didn't, I would say to myself, *Nope, not that one,* and by saying this, I had better results and it made my inner work easier. And, with time, I found my own ways of helping me stay in balance as much as possible with yoga, meditation, dancing, singing, going for a walk in the woods, and taking necessary time off from it all for a four-day weekend.

I learned that it was important to take the time to read and write during that weekend or simply sit back and receive from nature its magical energy that replenishes the body. I call this *taking a breather.*

Breathing To Release Emotions

Along the way I began to breathe. Yes, breathe consciously instead of shallow or short breathing or blocking it. I began using my breath, the exhale to be exact, to release the pain when I would hurt my toe on a piece of furniture or when I banged my elbow on the frame of a door. My technique is simple; breathe in deeply and connect to the pain, and as you exhale, exhale the pain with it. I did this a few times as the pain would subside, until it was gone.

One day I was divinely guided to use this technique for my emotions, and I was quite surprised by how well it worked. I was able to release my emotions through the exhale. If an overwhelming emotion arose, I would breathe into it until it went away, not even trying to know where it came from or what it was exactly. I simply *acknowledged it, breathed into it, and let it go.* It took some practice to let go of having to know what it was exactly or why it was there, but once I was able to do so, the process became easier and faster. What I loved about it was that I could do it anywhere, anytime, and people wouldn't even notice it. At times, if I needed to, I would go to the bathroom, lock the door, and do what I call *taking a breather*.

Finding Your Boat to Sail the Troubled Waters

It's so important for us to find our own way to release the overflow of emotions. Sometimes we need to try many different processes before we find the right one for us, always being aware that this can change over time as we evolve all the time. It can become a beautiful way of self-discovery at the same time. It can happen that some situations require different ways of releasing too.

It was important for me to be flexible about that and accept that there wasn't just one solution for all emotions. But I did find that the best way for me was *to be with* the emotions, not feel threatened by them, and release them. At times, I needed a very sturdy boat to sail these troubled waters; sometimes I needed a speedboat and other times, a simple sailboat was fine. So, after I had used the breathing technique, I would use *toning* sounds, which would help clear my energy and bring peace within. I can feel the shift every time.

The easiest one is *OM*, sung in a long, resonant tone. *OM* helps to clear the energies of the body and chakras, bringing us back into our centre. I also play with the sound, using lower and higher tones until I feel where it shifts in my body, and once I find the sound that moves the most energy, I sing it until I feel all has shifted. It can take just a few seconds or a few minutes, or I may need to repeat the process a few times to clear all that is there.

Drawing is another technique or *playing music*. The important thing is to experiment and see what feels the best for you; that is how

I found these ways to help me clear, live through difficult situations that brought intense emotions, and feel safe.

Rise Beyond and Above Troubled Waters

How many times do we hear people say *just let it go? You're wasting your time thinking of this.* These *clichés* don't help you in any way, or they simply make you feel the emotion more intensely or add a new one on top. Of course, we know it's well-intended, BUT it doesn't help us rise above and beyond troubled waters—those situations that bring us so much emotion. As I mentioned before, the breathing and the sounding help with the emotions once they're there, but when something is coming up or just beginning, how can we avoid feeling so torn and hurt inside?

Yes, *letting go* helps, but to get there, how or what can we do to achieve that? Many times I felt so puzzled and sad because I saw how easily others were able to clear things that bothered them or weren't affected by the events. It seemed so easy for them. Why not for me? Was it that I wasn't born with that gene of letting go, or was it something I hadn't learned as a child?

No matter what it was, I had to learn to let go, and it was hard at times just because I felt so vulnerable, as if I was letting someone down if I did that. Each time something would come up, like an event or a discord with someone, it brought another *letting go.* This meant I had to detach myself emotionally from the situation to be able to release it. As a highly-sensitive person, an empath actually, this is easier said than done.

How did I do it? I began with little things that didn't have a huge consequence on me or my life. Becoming conscious of my thought forms and patterns in small and even silly situations, even the funny ones, helped me to deal with it gently and effortlessly. I began to become more agile in detaching myself from the emotional situations. Thus, I was able to look at it with an outsider view, was able to bring things back into proportion, back to reality, and not from a highly emotional place.

It helped me to see more clearly what was really going on. Even if sometimes I still get caught up in a hurtful emotional situation, I give myself permission to feel the emotion, embrace it, breathe into it, and then take a step back. The best gift I could give myself was the permission *to be who I am*, acknowledge the feeling, and not judge what I'm feeling.

Establishing New Emotional Boundaries

Further down the road I learned something new. It was all nice and dandy to have all these new techniques to use, but if I didn't revisit my emotional boundaries, the same situations would arise and keep me in the loop of *What, I thought I had cleared this?* You know, those recurring patterns coming back to haunt you. I had to set new emotional boundaries, or just boundaries.

As far as I can remember, I always tried to please everyone, trying to make sure all were happy. I would forget about my own needs, my own emotions, what I really wanted. It became crucial for me to establish these new boundaries, healthier and respectful ones of myself and of others. Learning to say *no* at times or say, *I'll pass this time*. At first, I felt horrible, as if I was letting the entire world down. But in reality, I was putting myself first, and by respecting myself, I realized that I was more present for people, and I felt less pressure. A new type of freedom was beginning, and I could feel the lightness in my body.

Meditation

The Breath That Liberates

For you to be able to bring more peace into your life and liberate the overflow of emotions, the Divine Mother brings this meditation of Divine Breath. This breath is filled with all the divine qualities necessary to support you, hold you, and for you to feel safe while the work is being done. Divine Mother is working closely with your Divine Presence through this meditation. So please sit comfortably and ground your energies to the Earth's core and to Source.

Beloved One, as you breathe deeply, we come forth to you, embracing you, honouring you for your courage to come forth and ask for our assistance at this time in your life. We ask you now to breathe consciously into your heart, expanding it, then bring your breath into the Earth's heart, to your connection to the Earth. When you feel ready, breathe into your connection to Source. You are activating your connection, grounding your energy more deeply.

You are now lifted into a beautiful temple. We welcome you into Divine Mother's temple of love. Here all parts of you can feel safe, held, and supported. There is no judgment here, only love in its purest form.

Continue breathing consciously as you envision yourself entering this beautiful temple with its majestic doors of pink quartz. As you enter, you notice the crystalline floors and walls. You are invited to take place in the centre of the temple where you will sit on a beautiful crystal chair. Take notice of the pink colour of the chair. The colour of this crystal chair holds the frequency of the ray that will help you stay grounded fully and deeply connected to Source during this meditation.

We come to assist you in creating your own technique of breathing. We will teach you the basics of conscious breathing, which you can adapt to any situations or moments in your life. This can be done for a short period of time throughout the day or in a longer session so you can go more deeply in, clearing more of the emotions.

Concentrate on your breath. Inhale the love, grace, ease, and harmony. Exhale the emotions and old energies that no longer serve you. Do this exercise at least three times. Allow the breath to go where it is needed within you. You are guided and supported by the Divine Mother. She is there for you, holding you.

You do not have to relive the emotion to liberate it. See it as a TV screen without sound, with many images scrolling past. And with each breath, more and more of that loving energy fills you, and you begin to feel freer. You may continue breathing like this for ten to fifteen minutes if needed. When you feel the overflow of emotion has subsided, take a last inhale and exhale and give thanks for all that you have received at this time.

Divine Mother blesses you and thanks you for coming and allowing her to assist you at this time of change. Blessed be.

Note: Each time you do this exercise, it will be different as you will be working on something new each time. It will assist you in clearing some deeply rooted energies that you are not even conscious of at this point, and that is okay. Know that you are always supported; you only need to ask for help and assistance and you will have it.

CHAPTER 3

The Burnouts

Repetitive Events

Through life, there were repetitive events that occurred and everything that wasn't dealt with or healed within me had an impact. As these events were piling up, it became harder and harder to deal with them. Plus, the fact that I hadn't learned to say *no* to others—in case it might upset them or it was simply not nice to say *no*—added to the stress I felt. I was always giving more than my body could take, but I felt I had all the energy in the world and that it would never end.

After all, I wasn't working so hard. I had a desk job in accounting. I was happily married. I had met my husband after months of praying to God to put a man on my path so together we would evolve and be happy together. I kept saying to God, *You know me better than I know myself, so I trust you to find the perfect man for me.* I didn't know what type of man would be best for me, but I knew what I didn't want.

When I met him, I felt as if I had known him all my life. I had this deep profound *knowing* that he was an old, very old friend, and we talked all night. In the beginning of our relationship, I was afraid to open my heart fully to allow myself to be loved by him. He was extremely patient, loving, and caring, and finally I allowed myself to let him into my heart. The day of our wedding, I was so serene and sure of our union as we started our family life together. A first son was born four years after our wedding.

But because the early stages of my life were not entirely healed, or should I say barely healed, the unresolved grief, sadness, anger, and resentment from the consecutive or repetitive events of my childhood kept bringing up uncomfortable and unwanted emotions, which added more suffering inside my body, my mind. Memories swirled in my mind when new situations arose, and I dragged those memories into my current life: hospitalized for a major kidney infection at four years old, witnessing my father hit my mother and his repetitive shouting and cursing to anyone in the house. The sale of all the animals and farm equipment, the brutal divorce of my parents, seeing my mother in the hospital after her bad car accident, looking almost dead to me, my knee injury, my brother's death in a car accident, the death of my best friend's baby, the death of a school friend, always saying yes to other's wishes when I wanted to say no.

Add to this being laughed at. I was shy and an easy target for others. The list could go on, but remember all of these happened before I met my husband. It was a heavy load of unresolved emotions and energies. It came to a point where everything that didn't work out seemed like a loss, *everything*. Even things that flopped as simple as baking a pie, making a coffee, sewing a dress, or colouring an image would provoke outsized reactions. I had to have everything perfect the first time; this is what I had learned as a child. *For things to go smoothly, all had to be perfect. Those old memories were triggered by the smallest things going wrong.*

Conceiving our second child ended up being a four-year period of ups and downs, with a miscarriage in the middle of that. It's during those four years that I experienced the first burnout. When I got pregnant, the first five months were difficult. I had nausea and vomiting almost every day. I was so tired that my mother one day told me: *You look like a real zombie.*

I also had to be careful as the doctor said it was a previa, meaning the placenta is first. This can bring many complications at birth, but luckily it resolved itself before the term of the pregnancy was done. To add to all this, just before our second child was born, my stepfather died, and my husband lost his job. I was eight months pregnant, on a two-year sabbatical maternity leave negotiated by the union where I worked. This meant two years without pay and complete uncertainty about what was coming up for us.

I still remember looking at the birds outside while doing the dishes and saying to myself, just like a mantra, God never lets a bird die from hunger. God won't let us down. Those were difficult times economically, emotionally, and mentally, but we managed. At this point, my husband decided to start his own company, so we moved on. Jokingly we say we had twins at that time, a baby boy and a company.

Once the two years of maternity leave were over, I went back to work. All seemed to be going smoothly. Then, after a while, I began to feel that everything I did throughout my days at work and even at home was always very demanding on my energy level. My body was not keeping pace. Not only did I work all day, but I went home to care for my family. Then, as soon as the kids were in bed, I sat down to do our company's paperwork.

Soon, I noticed I would tire easily. I would need more and more sleep, plus I began to have migraines to a point where I had them every week starting from Wednesday until Saturday. It was excruciating pain, and no medication was helping entirely except the one prescribed to me, which my body got used to and started to create an addiction to.

It got to a point where the migraines were so bad that I had to quit my job. That same month, we got the news that my mother-in-law had cancer. Because my husband is an only child and his father had already passed, we were the only ones to care for her while she was in the hospital, and within eight months she had died.

Accumulated Pains and Sufferings

Because the consecutive and some repetitive events that were added to my repertoire brought more accumulated pain and suffering, it left me feeling even more tired as the grief was not entirely resolved, and I was continuing to run on low energy. I started my days tired and finished them exhausted. I had no time to care for myself with two young children at home and a company to run with my husband. Survival mode kicked in.

How did I survive after all these difficult events? I ignored the pain and the emotions and I developed ways of coping to survive. Withdrawing within, silence was my best ally. *If I don't talk to anyone, I am not connecting to the pain and the exhaustion; and therefore, I don't have to deal with it.* I kept pushing myself. I was my worst judge as I would tell myself *Others do it, so can you.* I could even hear my dad's voice in the back of my head saying, *Come on, don't be so lazy, just get up and do it.* So, I kept on going. After all, I was strong.

After many years of trying to have a third child, another huge disappointment, we decided to adopt. There were two reasons for us to adopt: one was because my husband always wanted to adopt, and after our second son I said, *Okay, let's adopt*. The second reason was I was not able to get pregnant, and after many tests and surgical intervention, we discovered I had only a 5 percent chance to conceive.

A new horizon opened up as we contacted the federal department for international adoption in Canada. We received a long document containing the list of countries and their prerequisites to adopt. With the list in hand, we began listing which country would allow us to adopt. Some countries have very specific demands, such as having to be completely sterile, not having any children, or being within a certain age range, to name a few.

So, from the countries we were allowed to apply to, we looked into South America as I speak a little bit of Spanish. But then on the news, there was a documentary about children being abducted from their mothers to be sold for adoption. We were outraged, and I said, *Never will I deprive a mother of her child*. So South America was crossed off our list.

So, we went back to our list. Because my husband *really* wanted to adopt a child from India, we tried with that country, but it didn't work. As we went through the list of countries again, at least three or four times, there were a few countries left in which our situation corresponded with their specifications. Vietnam was one of them, but we ignored it, even if many times it seemed like the ideal place. We had never heard about adoptions in that country, and we didn't know anyone that had adopted in Vietnam.

So, we tried with China. We contacted the person in charge of one adoption agency in Montreal, and the lady was straight-forward with us and told us *because you already have two boys, your file will end up at the bottom of the list.*

Once more we started looking into the list, and then I told my husband, *You know what, Vietnam keeps coming up each time we look at the list. I have a feeling our daughter is there.* We contacted the agency for the adoptions in Vietnam and applied there.

As I kept on going with the adoption process, things kept coming our way; a recession was in the brew. No one knew that yet but, in our business, it was becoming difficult to get contracts. We felt secure as we pulled together and organised all that was needed to keep our business afloat.

During the process of adoption, which took only nine months, I had put all the efforts necessary to have the documents required by the Vietnamese authorities and Canada ready as soon as possible, and we prepared for my departure to Vietnam. We also prepared all the documents and paperwork needed for our company while I was away. We made sure nothing was left undone. I was leaving for a minimum of two weeks, which ended up being three. While I was away, our five-year business success, our thriving industrial automation company, came to a halt.

The same week I got back home from Vietnam with our beautiful baby girl, we had to shut down our business to avoid bankruptcy. The recession had begun. Companies were not hiring outside help to retrofit their machines. The beautiful world we had built was crumbling down faster than I could pick up the pieces. I was devastated by this and had to deal with an addition to the family who wouldn't stop crying unless she was continuously in our arms. Plus, she would barely sleep. Again, I ignored all the signs of fatigue and kept on going while ignoring my own personal suffering of shutting down our dream business.

Meanwhile, my mother had some health issues, for which she was diagnosed only a few years later. Then I got pregnant. I had the feeling this child was going to have Down syndrome. I knew people who had children with Down syndrome; their children were attracted to me, and I truly enjoyed their company. But during the beginning of this pregnancy, I felt uneasy each time Down syndrome was mentioned, even during a documentary.

I began to understand that something unusual was going on and decided to have a chat with the soul of the child growing inside me. I knew deep down in my heart that I would not be able to care for this child the way it needed. I explained that with three children already, plus a mother slowly losing her physical capacities, I would not be able to care properly for it. It was too demanding for me, and I would probably go into depression. I knew myself enough not to lie about this. This chat happened on a Monday night, and on that Friday, the miscarriage happened. I was grieving this child and at the same time, I was honored that this soul had such love and respect for me and respected my request.

After a while, life was going well, and we decided to adopt again. Our fourth child would also be from Vietnam, so our girls would have a sense of belonging. We began the process again with the same adoption agency. This time it took two years before we were able to go and get our second daughter. During those two years, I had my third miscarriage. This one was hard. The twelve weeks were done, yet the contractions were just like at childbirth. I cried a lot. I created a little ritual on my own to say goodbye to the soul who had chosen not to come with us.

I kept this grief to myself as people were saying, *It's okay; you are adopting.* Then our second adoption in Vietnam was about to happen when my mother received her diagnosis of Parkinson's disease. Being a natural caregiver, I wasn't going to let her down; after all, she had always been there for me throughout my life. It was the right thing to do. I was only giving back what she had given me.

When we returned from Vietnam with our second daughter, my mother was referred to a long-term care hospital. Her case had gotten much worse, and she needed a lot more care in a day than any of us could provide her. Caring for a parent while dealing with four children at home with some teenage angst wasn't always easy. Some days coming back from the care centre where my mom lived, I felt devastated. I was witnessing her dying slowly. It was difficult and many times I wanted to cry, but as soon as I would get home, reality was awaiting with my rebellious teenager. I had no time to take care of myself. Again, I was exhausted, emotionally drained, and felt lost, but I didn't listen to my body. I became anemic.

About five years after receiving her diagnosis of Parkinson, my mother died. I had given so much to all that I had no energy left for me, and the second burnout had begun. But with the funeral and all paperwork that followed my mother's passing, I still wasn't listening to the signs of fatigue. I continued on as if nothing was happening. Because I was ignoring the exhaustion and emotional distress, my body accelerated the growth of a fibroma in my uterus. It was clear I had to go for surgery because it was seventy times the size of my uterus. Because of that, the flow of my periods became more abundant, thus making me even more anemic.

Fasting Because Of An Overload of Emotions

So much had happened all at once, one thing after the other, that I could barely keep up with all of it. I started to eliminate what I could to cope, to make time to care for the others. I was piling up the emotions because you cannot assist another if you are not smiling and happy, but the emotions were still there. I could feel them but chose to ignore them as much as I could.

Sometimes the emotions would rise to a level I couldn't deal with, and it would put my stomach into a knot so tight I couldn't eat. There was an overload of emotions that made my stomach feel so full I only nibbled here and there. Water was enough at times. Other times, I would realize I had not eaten or had anything to drink during the day, so I forced myself to eat a little to avoid fainting, but just nibbles. Until one day I was conscious another burnout had started, and I had to face this truth again. I was emotionally and physically exhausted; I had no energy left.

Giving Too Much Exists?

I am so tired, I would say, *not even a good night's sleep helps. I would love to live on a deserted island just to rest. What is going wrong? What is wrong with my body? Why won't it follow my pace? I have a lot to do; I can't stop. What about my children, my husband, and all the others who need me, and I have so much to do? There is always someone who needs my help!* I would shout in my head. *Stupid body, why can't you function like other people's bodies, like my husband who has so much energy all the time?*

Everyone had always told me I was slow. *I'm starting to believe it now. Look at me, I can't even accomplish the simple tasks of the household.*

What am I doing wrong? That was my inner dialogue; plus, the remarks my father used to say to us when we were young joined in: *You're so lazy. You're too messy.* Or, *come on, do it! You have to do it, or else.* Then my own head talk would say: *See, you can't even accomplish this.* This inner dialogue was in no way going to get me out of the loop, but it was persuasive.

I have always been a giver. I always gave gifts and time to everyone around me, to my family and friends, as a volunteer at the school library, our boys' soccer team, the adoption agency, and even the palliative care unit of the hospital. I thrived on this; I felt alive, I had a purpose, and I made people happy. Of course, I was creating a pattern for them not to try to do things on their own but to instead ask me first. So, it was easier for them while it was burning me out.

It never occurred to me that I was giving too much, not even during the burnouts, until I read the book *The Indispensable Woman* by Ellen Sue Stern. I was so surprised reading this book because even not paying the bills to gain a bit of time was in there. But what shocked me the most was this sentence: *The burnout is the step just before depression.* That got my full attention, as I had memories of how my mother was in her depression, and I didn't want to go there. That was a big no-no for me.

I had to do something about it, but what? With this book I started to realize I was giving too much. Really, *giving too much* exists? I had to go through the second burnout to understand this, and that was a painful lesson. I realized I had given so much that I had completely forgotten about my own need for rest, about myself, and had identified as only a caregiver. That is when my old belief systems came out and so did the emotions. I realized I had lost myself through giving too much.

Eating To Fill the Void

When all the emotions come out, sometimes you're left with such a big void inside you. I wasn't prepared for this, nor knew about how this can affect you, and I started to eat. I was hungry, but soon that turned into *if there is an emotion or something brewing inside me, I eat.* Sweets were best—fast food, junk food, chips, you name it. I would eat them and felt good at that moment, but right after, I would have a sugar crash.

It took some time before I realized what was going on and that even if I tried to control my eating habit, it would not stop. But it was there, and I sometimes felt guilty about my eating habit. I realized I needed to break this habit before my health declined. It wasn't an easy process. It took some time and will to change those habits; it was a long road. Now when food beckons, this has become an alert that something isn't going well inside of me, and it's time to help myself.

When Your Mind Halts and Stays on Pause

There came a time when nothing worked anymore, especially my mind. The emotional suffering of past events was weighing heavier and heavier on my heart, and it felt like my mind stayed on pause for a while; sometimes it was almost like a complete halt. People would talk to me, and it was not registering. I heard them, but because it was not registering, I had to ask them to repeat what they had just said. It made me uneasy many times, especially with new people.

For example, they would tell me their names, and I would look at them and could not repeat their name at the end of a sentence. It was like I was not living in my physical body. My body was functioning, but my mind could not follow the pace anymore. I thought I knew all the signs to prevent a burnout. But because this was more from an emotional aspect of fatigue, not physical like my first one, I did not foresee this possibility. The red flag was raised by my internal detectors, my intuition, that inner voice that says something is wrong. My intuition and inner guidance were the only way to protect my sanity. I was disconnected from my being.

Survive After Disconnecting from Your Being

How did I survive now that I was disconnected from my Being? I was not entirely disconnected, but it was enough to not want to do anything. I felt that everything was pointless, and again, my inner dialogue started. *What's the point; who cares anyway? Nothing good will come out of this. Nobody sees me. I am just like an old piece of furniture in the house. All they care about is getting what they want.* This went on and on for quite some time. I tried to quiet down this voice in my mind, so I watched TV. Yup, watching TV is perfect for a numbed mind; you just sit there watching others play roles while your life is slipping by. I was so exhausted that I could barely move or do anything. It was too hard to even try.

To tell you the truth, I felt exhausted when I would just *think* of all the things that needed to be done. Going out to see friends? *Oh, it will be too difficult to just go and come back, so why bother?* I stayed home. Day after day, I was building this hiding place that no one knew about, and smiling at people became horrendous. I was starting to withdraw from society. But it happened at times that someone would notice something was wrong with me. I slowly stopped calling even the friends I was calling in the beginning for support and who would listen to me. I felt like a broken record repeating myself all the time, and they had no solution for me. I began to think, *What's the use? They don't get it either.*

The Old Adages That Irritate

Sometimes there are these beautiful souls that come and notice you are suffering, and they so desperately want to help you, and then they serve you one of those trite pre-made statements that irritate you. I knew they meant well, but please give me a break here. *If I had a sore foot, it was because I did not want to move forward.* No, this foot was injured many years ago. *If my liver was clogged up, I had too much anger stored there.* No, I have some food intolerances and a slow gall bladder. *If my ear was hurting,* some would say, *What is it you don't want to hear? Having difficulty with your child or anyone, for the matter of fact? Oh, it is karma you two have.* or even better, *This is your mirror; you have the same in you.* P-L-E-A-S-E!!! Stop! Or others saying, *Oh, give it time. All will get better. You'll see; you are strong.* No, I'm not, can't you see how low I feel at the moment? *You have to give yourself time to heal.*

Enough with these ridiculous adages! They might work when people are well but not when you are down on the floor, flat in energy, anemic, or like I felt—a complete shadow of myself. They are aggravating more than anything else and irritating when we feel this way. What I really needed was to work with someone, a special person with whom I was extremely comfortable with, to allow myself to open up to my emotions and needs. I needed to find the one person who would help me find my way again back to myself.

I shopped around and made some phone calls. If I was going to pay someone, it had to be someone I had full confidence in. Someone I was willing to tell the truth about me, about what was *really there* deep down within me, so I could reconnect to myself gently and not be forced to do anything I did not want to do or found uncomfortable. I found this person; she was a social worker.

Who am I? Where am I?

Throughout the sessions, I realized I didn't know who I was anymore, I couldn't recognize myself, and I felt I did not have any identity anymore. The woman I once was, was no more. This woman I was reconnecting to was hurting so much and needed to unload. It seemed that all I had learned in life did not exist anymore. I had to dig it out bit by bit, and it would come out not on my terms but when I was ready for it. As much as my mind wanted to move things along, make progress, and allow my knowledge to resurface sometimes, it still did not come out. I had to be patient. Yes, I have always been patient. *Hmmm, not anymore—patience has sailed*. I had to learn to be patient again.

Then came the question of what I wanted to do. I had no answer to that as that was not easy either. I did not know who I was anymore, nor did I know where I was at in my life. How could I say what I wanted when I didn't know myself anymore? Nothing was the same; I was not the same person anymore, especially after my mother passed away. I had to reinvent myself.

Getting Out of the Physical and Mental Lethargy

To help my physical body get back into shape—because that too had gone through the window—I decided to work with a health coach. It was difficult to do some self-care because the migraines showed up again every week. This time, I was determined to get rid of them once and for all. After forty years of migraines, it was time. If I added up all the days I spent in bed with one of those, which ended with me throwing up, I had spent over a year in bed with migraines.

With my new coach and friend, I started to learn about self-care and getting back to exercise. I barely had enough energy to get me through my days, so forget about exercise. She told me, *Out you go. Go walk to the corner of the street if that's all you can do.* She told me that I had to do it just to break the vicious circle of fatigue I was in, along with learning what to eat and not to eat.

I was discovering a lot about myself and my physical body. Three months into our coaching, I had no more migraines, I was able to take long walks, slept better, and stayed awake during the day. I was not dragging myself around anymore to *do* my days. With this wonderful friend-coach, I gained my life back. Now I swim 1200 meters easily, three times a week. She showed me a way back to my physical health and clarity of mind.

Meditation

Regeneration of the Bodies and Energies

To be able to regenerate your energy, you must take the time to recentre and bring all your energies back into alignment, even the ones that have been scattered around. When you're a giver, you tend to give without limits until your own energy is flat. To assist you in regenerating your energy, I have received this guided meditation from the Angelic Mothers, Ancestral Mothers, and their assistants.

As you sit down in a relaxed position, close your eyes and take three deep breaths. Bring your attention to your heart centre and ground your energy to Mother Earth. Allow the energy of the Earth to move up through your chakras, filling each part of your body with an energy of love and strength that uplifts your energy level.

Each breath you take brings in more and more of that love-energy. Now that you have taken in some of that wonderful energy, concentrate on your in-breath to take in that energy from the Earth. And at the exhale, allow all the energies that do not serve you anymore to flow back to the Earth's core to be transmuted with the violet flame. A team of Angelic Mothers and Ancestral Mothers are there to support you and assist you in this process.

At that point, you begin to feel calmer and can now call in all the energies which you have been scattering around. Call back all of your energy you have left here and there, even unknowingly. Allow it to come back to you so you may replenish your energy. This is done while you are still breathing consciously.

Now that you have regathered your energy, call to an Angelic Mother to assist you in recalibrating your energy field, re-attuning it to the universal energy field. As they recalibrate and rebalance your energy field, the Ancestral Mothers come and clear your physical body, your ancestral body, and your elemental body of all blocks in the flow of your energy so you may feel energized more rapidly, which will ease the flow of energy through your bodies and help you to stay energized for longer periods of times.

Receive and release old energies, receive the love and strength energies, and let them fill you, and with your next breath, allow these energies to fill your auric field, making you feel stronger with each breath you take in.

*Each breath you take brings in
more and more of that love-energy.
Now that you have taken in some of that
wonderful energy, concentrate on your in-
breath to take in that energy from the Earth.
And at the exhale, allow all the energies that
do not serve you anymore to flow back to
the Earth's core to be transmuted with the
violet flame. A team of Angelic Mothers and
Ancestral Mothers are there to support you
and assist you in this process.*

From your heart centre, allow your Higher Self to come and pour forth the love, peace, and light energies. Open your heart to these energies. Give permission for this; give permission to your Higher Self, your Divine Presence, to fill your heart, your body, and your mind with the divine energies of love, peace, and light that will enhance your energy level. Know that each time you fill your heart like this, it is much easier for you to emanate love and light with ease and grace.

Now take the **Code:** *Regeneration of the Bodies and Energies* and look into it; allow it to imprint all your chakras. Allow it to flow into each of your chakras. It activates and releases all energies and blocks that no longer serve you and activates your natural flow of energy, aligned with your Divine Energy and the unified field of the Earth. This will leave you feeling fully replenished and peaceful.

As the Metatron cube spins in your chakras, you can feel the joy uplifting. All your chakras begin to release the lethargic energies and vibrate to the frequency of joy again. Just like a breath of fresh air reinvigorates your body, this Code elevates your frequency in divine joy and assists you in the expansion of your energy field.

Sing the mantra twelve times (12X) in long, resonant sounds, which will awaken all parts of you that are asleep so you can go deeper in the clearing and activating of the energies. This process can be repeated three times a week, no more, and allow a day in between each activation to give your body time to adapt and settle in with these higher frequencies.

Feel the transformation that occurs in your physical body, your mind and your heart. Journal to keep track of your progress.

REGENERATION OF THE BODIES AND ENERGIES

Nicole Kishalah 2020

MAYA KARI NA MO (12X)

CHAPTER 4

The Field of Doubt

The Indecisive Way

How many times have I stood in life filled with doubt? It has been a companion for a long part of my life, and it even directed me many times and on many levels. It is exhausting to doubt all the time, always bringing things you have done in the past back to your mind to question them, not knowing which way to turn. At times, it felt as if I had so many avenues I could take. It felt like I was standing in a field of fully grown crops of corn. I could go this way, that way, or this other way.

At times, I felt as if I was on the right path, but then, doubt crept in, and I would go back, only to realize that I was not where I started from. Which, of course, also made me doubt even more the decisions I had taken! Other times, the paths were very clear, but I felt as if I was not ready. I was doubting my abilities to make the right decision. Doubting can be scary and frustrating. You simply don't know which way to go, and we all have our own way of dealing with doubt.

Procrastination: This False Ally

One of my ways to deal with doubt, especially when needing to make a choice in life, such as *Should I take this job or not? Should I accept that promotion or not? I know I need to change something in the way I do things, but* ... I would go into procrastination mode. Procrastination gave me that false sense of *I am still safe*, the change hasn't happened yet, there is no need to change anything in my life, or any other reason I would give myself to avoid making a choice or doing something that meant going into insecurity. As long as I procrastinated, I felt somewhat safe. I knew exactly how the game was played in my life, even if it made me feel uneasy or even miserable. At least I knew those rules, until the day came when it was completely unbearable. To survive and become who I really am, I needed to say goodbye to my false ally, Procrastination.

Losing One's Points of Reference

When I took the plunge into the unknown, turned around, and chose myself, it felt as if I was completely lost. I had completely lost my points of reference in life. All that used to work before no longer did, and I had no idea of what needed to be done or where to turn. I felt completely lost not knowing who I was anymore or what I wanted, so it was impossible to know what I wanted to do next.

It felt as if I was in a reboot mode. I had cleared the old thought processes, had made space for the new, and now that I had all that space within, I thought, *What do I do with it?* Things that seemed easy before became difficult, and mostly I did not recognize myself in that new space.

It felt as if I was in a reboot mode.
I had cleared the old thought processes,
had made space for the new, and now that
I had all that space within, I thought,
"What do I do with it?"

Where am I? Looking at Yourself and Asking Yourself Questions

I often asked myself questions about where I was at, where I wanted to go, or what I wanted to do, and these questions ran through my head in an incessant, never-ending loop. My mind was never at ease because of those questions. *Why do I have so many questions?* I would wonder. I was looking around, and all my friends and coworkers seemed to know where they were heading in life, and I had no clue.

I kept asking the Universe over and over, *Why do I feel this way? Why do you, Universe, leave me on my own like this? Why do I feel so alone, even if I am surrounded by so many people? Why can't I get this like the others? Why is my path so bumpy and unclear?* The questions kept rolling in until I chose to sit and be with myself for a little while and really see what was there inside of me, what was really going on in my head. I had to face myself and wasn't sure I would like what I found, especially because at the time I felt so unsure and lost.

Experiencing Emptiness Within

Once I actually looked at myself in the mirror, so to speak, I began to feel empty, and that was a moment when I felt the lowest and alone. It was so difficult to experience this emptiness, especially when I was surrounded by family and friends. I would look at them, notice them, but I had no conversation, no thoughts—just this immense void inside that kept screaming. Soon, I would avoid going out because I had nothing to say or share. I thought no one would understand what I was feeling because I had a great husband and four wonderful children. My life seemed so wonderful from the outside, but this hollow space deep within me was all I could feel. But, I am a fighter and at some point, I started to fight back as I thought this was not the right path for me.

Should I Turn Back? But Where Would I Go?

Certainly not where I CAME from.

I was starting to make changes in my life once more—mostly within me, changing my thought forms when the fear crept in again. I started to doubt the choices I had made because I was so uncomfortable. That is when I started to believe I should get back to how things were as it seemed easier, and I felt much happier then, than now . . . or so I thought. I realized that it was only my imagination trying to trick me into going back to my old ways, the ways my mind knew how to deal with. Even if it was not the best situation, at least I knew how to deal with it and how to go about it.

Only I had forgotten how difficult it had been to go back there. It's just like having to change your old shoes that used to fit so well but are worn out and give you pain at the end of the day. We reluctantly go buy a new pair. At first, we love them, they seem comfortable, until we have worn them all day and our feet hurt a little. Also, because it is a different pair of shoes, we think that *they* are the cause of the pain. In fact, it is only a question of time for the shoe to stretch to the shape of our foot, but we need to remember that until then, they might hurt a little. Because they hurt, we may be tempted to go back to the old shoes that were so comfortable but gave us leg or back pain, simply because we know how we feel inside those old shoes. The pain with the new shoes is different; the feet hurt a little but without the leg and back pain.

It was explained to me that when I create changes in my life it is because what I was experiencing before did not bring me enough joy to compensate for the difficult times, the hardship. Thus, we begin making changes that make sense, and we believe that these changes will bring more joy. No doubt they do at the beginning because they are new, but the in-between time is the difficult place to be as we adapt to the new way of things, to the transformation within. These changes made me feel lost at times, but still the doubt was there; I was unsure what to do next or where to turn. I was completely confused and exhausted, and it was taking a toll on my emotional state.

The Tears of Liberation

If there would have been a thermometer to measure my emotional state, it would have burst at the top. My belief system was that *because I am a mother, I have to be there for everyone.* I was there to welcome all of my children back from school with all their physical baggage as well as their emotional baggage, then did the same for my husband and all the people who called me for comfort, but no one was there for me. Who would understand? I could hear what people said about people like me. *They have it all, and they complain.* My emotions kept going up and up in intensity until I burst into tears—big, ugly, sobbing tears which I thought would never end—and I could not understand how far deep inside of me the pain was coming from.

I cried often, but each time I started to feel better. I was liberated from this heavy weight on my heart. My entire body was feeling lighter and lighter, bringing a sensation of inner peace a little bit more at a time as I healed, and I was feeling good. The more I felt the peace within me, the more relaxed I became.

Soothing One's Mind

My mind was able to go into stillness more often, even if at times my mind was all over the place. I was careful not to judge myself. I was reading short articles about the transitions we go through in life and their impact on us—how these transitions can bring up old, not entirely resolved feelings. Knowing about these transitions helped me continue to bring changes in my life and in my belief systems. I owned that some of those feelings and my belief systems were obsolete and were not serving me, and I was not moving forward nor clearing recurring patterns.

All of this work/process was helping me to get out of that fog I felt in my mind at times, and I was giving myself permission to be who I was, *while learning who I am*. Music also helped soothe my mind and my heart. At other times, I would sing at the top of my lungs, even though I am not a great singer. I sang until I felt lighter. I learned that when the heart is at peace, the mind follows. I continued reading. What brought peace to my mind was discovering that I was not alone and that I needed to give myself a break from time to time. As they say, I needed to take the time to smell the roses.

Feeling more peace within helped me feel more fulfilled. It encouraged me to continue to move forward and bring more peace into my life. Moving out of doubt showed me that what I had always called *doubt* had different facets. Sometimes it is okay to doubt myself; that's what intuition is for, and I had to learn to work with it.

The Art of Hesitation

Although it took me a long time to accept and get to this point in my healing, I have learned to give myself permission to feel different or not okay with certain things, and it was good to take a longer time to make a choice. I started to learn the *art of hesitation*. I learned to hesitate intentionally to give myself the space and time I needed to process things and make a decision that would be best for me. This was contrary to how I made decisions in the past, to hesitate because I feared a certain result or outcome, or even a confrontation. When I hesitated under stress or fear, it was more a space where I was totally unsure or even paralyzed by the stress or the emotions attached to the situation.

You know when you are under stress and your brain goes blank or you can't focus or think clearly, and then people pressure you to make a decision and it elevates the stress in you? In these situations, I became impatient, and it made me angry. I rarely made the best choices for myself in those moments. But with the *art of hesitation*, I *intentionally* take a step back to have an overview of things. It also gives me a chance to detach from certain situations, control my emotions, and not get caught up in the drama of them so I can make a clearer and wiser choice.

At first, people were impatient with me for doing this. I put pressure on myself to make quick decisions because life was moving very fast, and we were very busy all the time. That pressure made me feel as if I had to perform just like an athlete. It seemed as if others were coping much better than me with situations, and I had to work hard to accept myself as I was and not to compare myself to others. After all, they were not living my life. I was hesitant in moving forward, hesitant to make changes, hesitant to make certain decisions and so on.

Once I was able to see and *know* the difference between real *hesitation* and *fear*, it became much easier to practice my *art of hesitation*. When I was fearful, I would become paralyzed and would be unable to act or say anything. This was an involuntary reaction on my part. It was as if I was frozen in time, but in the moment, I was trying to grasp all that was going on all at once. Then one day I discovered I could, in many situations, take a pause instead, breathe and allow myself to take the time to make a choice about what to do next or how to respond. Who hasn't hesitated making a decision or a change?

What I understood is when the hesitation to make a change or to make a choice was done from a feeling of fear, those choices rarely brought the best outcome. At that point, I started to give myself the permission to take some time, to reflect on what the impact was for me. I was giving myself the space to process the emotions flowing through me. This was the beginning of my intentional hesitation. I was hesitating in order to give myself the time and space to process my choices and decisions. I learned to do this out of respect for myself. Giving myself permission to hesitate voluntarily was a new beginning for me, a new step in finding my freedom to truly be me.

Regaining Your Power That has Been Scattered Around Through Years and Events

My power? *What power?* For many years I saw myself as powerless, afraid and always having to fight back to gain something. Life was a fight, and if someone came along and spoke louder or was more aggressive than I was, I would bow down and let them win. I grew up thinking that I was worthless. These beliefs brought me to believe that everyone else was more intelligent than I was. In addition, because I am the youngest of seven children, I felt everyone in my family knew more than I did, and that was the way we were brought up to think of ourselves, as worthless. That's the way it was in our house.

I was certain that success was not for me. Many people were much more than me, they had a better education and had degrees I did not have. Also, because I found it hard to say *no*, I would back down. I was a people pleaser. In other words, I was giving my power away to others, so I worked hard to regain this power of mine. I now understood that for me to feel whole, I had to get my power back.

But what was power? As a child, I thought strong people had power; people in higher positions or who spoke louder were powerful. Those people who were bold had power, and I feared them all because my limiting beliefs stated that I am weak, young, and a girl on top of that. As a teenager, I was teased because I came from the country; to some people, I was less than they were because they were from the big city. I did not dress like they did either. All this added up and made me feel less-than because I believed I was less than they were.

It was a long recovery from those beliefs. Then I learned the real meaning of power: my biggest power is the love I have for myself. To discover that I had to turn inward some more and redefine myself, not from past events, but from my truth. I realized that I had more emotional clearing to be done. At this point, you are probably wondering how much clearing had to be done. It was a lot.

I had so much clearing to do because I held everything within me, and all that I held inside me was not my truth, so these thoughts had to go. The best way to do that was through loving myself enough, by accepting myself not according to some standards of society or from what someone said, but to the truth of *who I really am*. This healing didn't happen overnight. Those clearings came in layers.

I learned different techniques, such as affirmations, prayers, working with Archangel Michael, and many other Beings of Light. Also, I learned about clearing emotional cords between me and another person, taking back what belonged to me, and giving back what belonged to them. I practised all I could to regain my power and feel whole again. I was on my way to another level of loving myself. I found that by reclaiming my power, I was able to change doubt more easily into something more positive.

Meditation
Turning Doubt Into Affirmation

Beloved One, we come to you at this time to assist you to clear doubt and release the thought-forms that are attached to it and to help you turn doubt into affirmations. What do we mean by that, you might ask? It is very simple Dear One. Each thought-form can be realigned in divine order with the pure intention of your heart and by mastering the art of your thoughts. We are the Council of Five and come to you today to teach and assist you with this simple and practical technique that you will practice through meditation. This type of meditation is very active as your mind will be busy watching what is occurring within your mind and emotions and also will be learning to differentiate the *doubts* from the *fears*. You will learn to recognize the doubts that are simply a hesitation in choice, versus the doubts that arise because of fear.

We now invite you to close your eyes and take a deep breath while bringing your attention to your heart centre and allowing the love that resides within your heart to expand. Continue breathing deeply and slowly for a few minutes. Bathe in this love-energy. Allow it to expand even more now, so your entire body is completely enveloped in it. Continue expanding so all your multiple bodies now can be filled with love-energy. Take a few more moments to breathe into this energy of love.

Once you feel that energy of love all around you, open your mind to the energy of love, inviting it to show you moments when you were in doubt, the times where you had a panoply of choices. There were simple choices to be made where you had a lot of different choices and where there were no difficult outcomes. You could make a pure and simple choice. Think of it as if you were at the fork of a trail and you have to choose to go left or right, and that no matter which way you go, there will be good results. Each choice creates a different result, but they are all good. Those choices are simply hesitations. Doubt arises when you lack confidence in your power of choice. Doubt means you fear making a bad decision, you fear the outcome, which in turn is only the fear of making a mistake.

Continue connecting to the energies and images your mind is giving you without judgment. Allow these images to flow through your mind. Now bring the energy of love into them. Allow the energy of love to fill in these images and the thoughts that come with them. See them transform with the love-energy, see them untangling for you to be able to have more clarity when facing a choice. Continue breathing into the love-energy and release all old energies that do not serve you anymore when faced with choices.

When you feel ready, call for the violet flame to activate in your heart and all your chakras. Breathe into it and intend for it to expand now for all your bodies to be filled with the violet flame, especially your mind and your emotional bodies. This violet flame will transmute all discordant energies and energies that blur your judgment when faced with a choice that brings up fear in you or uncertainty.

Breathe in the love-energy and the violet flame. See yourself as the love-energy and the violet flame. Continue breathing for a few more breaths and ask for the violet flame and the love-energy to flow through your emotional and mental bodies. Allow your breath to move these energies through your bodies. As the violet flame transmutes the discordant energies, the love-energy restores the flow of love within the bodies. Continue breathing whilst this is occurring within you and your bodies.

Your mind will become clearer through this process; the fears and the doubts are being untangled, released for your highest good and the highest good of all. Give thanks for all the transformations and transmutations that are occurring for you at this time.

Once this exercise is done, you can now take the **Code: Interdimensional Disc of Transmutation**, look into it, intend for it to enter your Third Eye chakra and activate itself as you begin singing the mantra thirty-three times (33X).

This Code will spin through the third eye and then move into the heart chakra, going into all chakras whilst you continue chanting the mantra in long resonant tones. Allow your heart to find the melody of it; your Divine Presence is assisting you.

As you sing the mantra, you can feel yourself becoming more peaceful and having more clarity. Once you are done singing, all ties, blocks, or thought forms that no longer serve you for your highest good have been removed and lifted, and the energy of love has filled in all these areas. You are becoming more and more confident. You begin to feel your inner strength. And you can now state: *I am confident and stand in my power. I am always assisted by my Angelic assistants, my Guides, and my Divine Council. I can now make choices from the centre of my heart and trust that I am held at all times. I can make choices from the energies of love and faith. I trust myself that I make the best choices for myself and for my highest good and the highest good of all. And so it is.*

INTERDIMENSIONAL DISC OF TRANSMUTATION

Nicole Kishalah 2020

ORA NE O MA (33X)

CHAPTER 5

The Island of Compassion

A Time-Out

With each moment of clearing, there were time-outs, times when all felt calm and stable, uneventful. It felt as if I could finally enjoy being who I am with my family. It was bringing some silence into my heart and stopping me from going from one activity to another, always being so busy. Giving myself the space, the time to be me, to be with me, letting myself be held by my Guides and my Divine Presence, helped me with my healing.

Sometimes I found these moments unproductive, when in fact they were the most productive ones because I was recharging my energy, refilling my heart with love, and nourishing my entire body and spirit. Allowing myself to be in that space brought a tremendous amount of new insights, new ideas that I did not even think possible before—so many new possibilities.

Those time-outs were so necessary after the burnout and yet, exceedingly difficult at first for the overachiever, the perfectionist that I was. I had to learn to sit down and do nothing; that was unconceivable to me, and my body had said enough of this nonsense. A wonderful being helped me to take the time-outs necessary during the day and that was my cat, Henrietta. She would come begging for me to pick her up and pet her, and gently, very gently, she guided me to be in the moment while she was on my lap. At the beginning, fifteen minutes felt like hours to me, but with time it became easier, and she made sure I would take the time every day to sit with her. I was unknowingly going back into meditation; going back deep into my heart to rest for a while. My body was in time-out, but my mind was not following as easily as my physical body.

Resting

There are different ways to rest. There is a good night's sleep or a nap during the day in your favourite chair or on the train home after work, but when you have gone beyond your energy level, into exhaustion and burnout, that is not enough. Little time-outs had helped, but now that I could reach into my heart, I needed to rest there, to stop entirely and *be* there, learning to live with myself. At some point, it meant I had to stop working entirely to give myself, my body, and my mind the rest it needed. A two-week vacation would not do it. My soul needed a deeper process of reconnecting.

More guided meditations were on the menu, as well as observing life and everything around me, as well as being totally present in the moment. Choosing to do less in a day and respecting my limits were new processes for me. Giving myself permission to be resting at any time during a day whenever it was needed was new to me. Recharging my energy before the children would come back from school was a priority. By changing my order of priorities, I was able to rest and let myself be in the arms of my Angels and to give them permission to assist me on all levels.

Accompanying the Dying: My Greatest Teachers

At some point I was guided to a book that talked about assisting the dying. That just made my heart sing. I did not want to work a 9-to-5 job in a closed environment anymore. I had this profound inner knowing that I was to resign from my position, and one morning I woke up and knew that this was the day. When I got to work, I told my boss that I was quitting my accounting job, knowing fully that I was being guided towards my heart's wish—accompanying the dying on their final journey. I had no idea how or when this would happen, but I did feel this deep calling in my being.

I allowed the events to unfold, always asking God to guide me if accompanying the dying was my path. To my surprise, the first person I accompanied was my mother-in-law. What a gem she was. With her, I learned a few things about being fully present in the moment and what was important as a woman, a mom, a wife, a daughter, and all the roles I played in life. She taught me the greatest respect of each Being just by allowing me to be there for her. She helped me confirm that this is what I wanted to do—accompany the dying.

A few months after my mother-in-law died, a woman heard about how I accompanied my mother-in-law and wanted to talk to me. When I called her, she suggested that I call the psychologist in charge of the volunteers in the Palliative Care Unit of the Royal Victoria Hospital in Montreal. After a few meetings with the psychologist, I became a volunteer in the palliative care unit of this hospital. I was living my heart's desire, but inner peace did not always come easily. I had to face certain fears I did not know about, especially my fear of the unknown.

As some of the patients were living their last days, there were also families living through their own grief. The doctor in charge of the palliative care unit had given all new volunteers training about how the process of assisting them worked, what we were allowed to speak about, what was not allowed, what was expected of us, and also, that we had the choice to say no if the work became overbearing for us.

One sentence this doctor said stuck with me. He said, *Remember, as the family members are saying goodbye to their loved one, this patient is also saying goodbye to each and every one of their family members and loved ones.* This brought everything into perspective for me. I was to stay attentive to that point.

With an open heart, I began my volunteering and was assigned to go with the music therapist to assist her with another volunteer. I had imagined so many scenarios of what I would be doing on my first day, but never in my wildest dreams would I have thought I would be asked to sing then told by the patient that I was out of tempo!

Because I am highly sensitive, I began to ask God to help me to be guided in my actions and my words. I did not know these people and felt I was coming into their life in their most vulnerable moment. Guidance would help me a lot in many different moments.

There came a day when I was asked to sit with a lovely gentleman I had the honour to meet before. He was in his last days at that point. The nurse asked me if I was okay to sit next to him, keeping an eye on him in case he would begin hemorrhaging or choking. Suddenly, the fear of choking came up in me, and I was on the verge of saying *no* when I paused and took my *moment of hesitation* to think about it, to tune in and receive my guidance, and I said *yes*. I sat there nervously at first. I kept talking to my Guides for assistance. I used a long and deep breathing technique to breathe through my fear and let it go. Soon enough I was comfortable enough to relax and sit for the thirty minutes I was assigned for.

One other day, I offered a patient to go outside. If she wanted to I could bring her in a wheelchair. She replied, *No, I don't want to go because you volunteers always have to talk and talk and talk, and I don't want to talk.* With a loving voice I replied, *If what you want is not to talk, I'm all good with that. We don't have to talk at all. We'll just sit there quietly.* She turned to look at me, surprised, then decided to go out as long as we did not speak. I said, *Fine with me!* We went outside, enjoying the sunshine and looking at the squirrels going back and forth. Suddenly, she opened up about her life and talked to me for more than an hour. Unknowingly, I had given her the space for her to open up, simply because I had respected her wish for silence. I had so many conversations with the patients, their families, and other people there. Many of those conversations were amazing.

What Dying People Taught Me

Some of the patients helped me discover that I was there for a reason, to assist them in the final moments of their precious lives. At the same time, they were helping me learn to enjoy the present moment by not taking anything for granted, and mostly not to dwell on things that happened. Others taught me the importance of loving, of enjoying life and to participate in life as it is happening—for me to not always be on the go, but instead to take the time to *be*. I learned to walk with an open heart and be fully present to the person in front of me. Others brought confirmations to questions I had in my heart and without me saying a word about it, they would comment on something which brought me answers. I felt in sync with life itself, with the Divine working through me.

The biggest lessons they taught me were to love myself beyond all, to open my heart without limit, to surrender to what is in the moment, and that God is always with me. With their help, I was able to walk with an open heart and allow the energy that was for them to pour through my heart, to their hearts.

Rebirthing Myself

All these processes helped me rebirth myself with more ease as I felt safe in my heart. Not that it was a new me entirely, only that I was becoming conscious of who I truly was. I was discovering the truth of my heart. My soul was present with me. I felt the connection to myself, and I embraced it. I was opening up to new levels of consciousness and the best part of my heart.

Elevating Yourself to Attain the Depth of Your Being

As I went deeper and deeper within, I was able to connect to the real me and raise my vibrations and my frequencies so I could connect to the deepest parts of me that were hurting. I was able to connect to the deep parts of me that wanted to come alive and to all that love and wisdom within me. With some meditations, healing sessions, and prayers, I was able to reconnect more to myself each time I took the time to sit with myself and ground my heart's flame to the Earth, to the Divine within me. Also, calling for assistance from the Archangels,

Ascended Masters, Angels, and any other Beings of Light was key for me to open to myself in a new way.

Things had to change for me to be able to bring myself back to love and to my heart. I worked with different modalities, mostly Archangel Michael's teachings with his pyramid of light, by listening to guided meditations, using visualizations, and writing affirmations as well as connecting to my Guides and receiving wisdom from them that would help me to reach deep within, deeper than I had ever gone before.

You will find different modalities work best for you, and it is important to be able to resonate with the tools you use so you will get the best outcome for yourself. If it did not make my heart happy, I would not do it. It's okay to try many different ones. I sure did, and I was able to identify what worked best and resonated well with me.

Toning (sounding) is one of the ways that helps bring my energy back into alignment and raises my frequency very rapidly. I can feel the change in my body when it returns to centre. I also become calmer inside; both my heart and my mind become aligned.

Devoting Yourself to Yourself Now

Once I was able to bring myself back into alignment more easily, it was time to devote more time to myself. I was learning self-care. Oh! Did I ever feel selfish at the beginning! I, who was used to taking care of others and not think of my own needs, was coming first. But with time, it became obvious that self-care was not being selfish, it was being more responsible and respectful of my own being. I learned to say *no*. I was becoming more conscious of what I was feeling in different situations and learning when to say *yes* and when to say *no*. This is not always easy, you might say, but it is doable one step at a time. Every time you say *no*, the next time it is easier to say it. Being respectful of myself and devoting more time to myself helped me have more compassion towards myself and helped me with becoming empowered.

Finding Peace in Your Power

Now that I was more in touch with my true self, I was able to connect to my power. I had scattered my power around many times. But the more I connected to my deeper self, I was becoming more and more empowered. I started to call back all my power I had left here and there over the years. I allowed this to return to me, through my heart and by asking for assistance from my Guides, my Angelic team. The more I became conscious of my power and gave myself permission to acknowledge it, the more I was at peace.

Inner Communications with Angels, Your Soul, Your Divine Presence

Having inner communications was revealing to me. To have these conversations, I did a meditation, and while sitting, I would ask questions deep into my heart and listen to the answers from my Guides. Other times, I would journal or do automatic writing. I did what was working for me in the moment I was doing it. I was able to communicate with my Guides or the Angels while peeling my potatoes!

I have always cherished these intimate moments with the other world, my Guides, and the Angels. I have argued with them too. But one thing for sure is that they were always there for me and ready to assist if I gave them permission to do so for my highest good. They guided me through simple processes to engage in a deep conversation with my different aspects. These aspects are who I have been in another lifetime, another space or dimension. For you, my reader, some of these aspects may hold memories of losing your power or any other wounds or fears related to your power. It can happen that these fears, these wounds, can be at play in this lifetime, but they occurred during a different lifetime and are affecting your emotions in this life. This applies even to fears we are not aware of consciously.

The meditation that follows was channeled to help you open yourself to the love living deep within you. It opens the heart to your light and love and prepares you to receive from your higher self all the support you need to become conscious of your power, your divinity.

Meditation
Opening Your Heart to Love
and Compassion

As we come forth to you, we, the Angelic Mothers, invite you to connect deeply to your heart so you can rebirth to yourself and connect deeply to the Divine Love and the compassion within you. Here is a short meditation that will assist you in doing so. To us, the Angelic Mothers, we see you as a being of love and compassion, as we see you through the eyes of love and compassion.

As you sit quietly, breathe deeply a few times and allow your breath to connect to your heart. Allow yourself to fall deeply into your heart centre, this place within you that holds all the love and compassion. Do not worry about the thoughts that may arise; simply allow them to flow by just like a TV screen. Recognize that they are only thoughts at this point and will not interfere through this process.

As you go deeper within your heart centre, we invite you to call in your Divine Presence to assist you. We stand around you in a beautiful circle, radiating love through our hearts into yours. Welcome this love as it will bring you the support that you need at this time, to open more to the Divine Love and compassion that you hold deep within your heart. With this love and divine energy, you are now lifted into a beautiful crystal chamber where in the centre blazes a beautiful pink and violet flame. These two flames are connected today to assist you to clear and transmute old energies that do not support love and compassion and no longer serve you at this time in your life.

You are invited to take your place on a beautiful crystal seat. It is golden and pink and assists you to hold the frequency of love and compassion as it arises. Once you are seated on this beautiful chair, take the time to breathe in a few times these magnificent energies that are flowing through you. Give yourself permission to feel the love and compassion that begin to accentuate and expand in your heart. Continue breathing; the breath is key in this process. It helps you to stay connected to your heart and also helps liberate what is no longer needed on your journey.

Now that you begin to feel the expansion of your heart, we invite you to connect to the Angelic Mother who stands in front of you. She brings you a gift to assist you to release and let go of old thought forms and patterns that no longer serve you. She asks you to give her all that has been hurting your heart, all that has brought you to closing your heart to yourself.

Take your time with this process. Your Divine Presence is there with you. Also, two golden Angels come and stand on each side of you to assist you and hold you for each time you felt alone, abandoned, or not supported. They are here to help you to release those beliefs as you feel their presence on each side of you. They come from the Pleiades and hold the wisdom of the heart, the wisdom of knowing one's connection to their own heart, to their love and compassion. These two Angels assist you in going deeper within your heart, to help you release old stories of not being loved nor being love, stories of not being compassionate.

As these two Angels help you hold the frequency through this process, the Angelic Mothers begin to clear the pathways of your heart and your mind that are linked or connected to these thought forms, the beliefs, stories, and patterns that have been reoccurring in your life and lifetimes. Continue to give away all that comes up for you; the Angelic Mother is still there in front of you, taking it all so you can feel free from all these pains. Breathe deeply as the clearing of the pathways of your heart and mind is being done. Give yourself permission to receive this. Continue receiving all the beautiful energies of love and compassion along with the clearing energies.

Once you feel this is done, the Angelic Mothers invite you to step up to the pink and violet flames in the centre of the crystalline chamber. You are now invited to step into this beautiful flame of love and transmutation. As you step in, you can feel the refreshing, cooling effect of these two flames. They are now clearing your entire body and energy fields of discordant energies and enhancing your frequency as well as recalibrating it. Stand in that flame a little longer and allow it now to rebalance all your bodies together. You will feel the strength of the love-energy and of compassion becoming stronger within you. The more you connect to it, the stronger you will feel and the more you will be able to connect easily to your heart centre and stay connected for longer periods of time too.

When you feel complete, you can step out of the flames and come back to your crystal chair. This is where now you will begin to work with the Code that you have. This Code will assist you to open and expand your heart and feel more easily the love and compassion that is within your heart.

Look into the **Code: *Opening the Heart to Love and Compassion*;** bring it in through your third eye, and let it come down into your heart chakra and begin to sing the mantra twenty-two times (22X). Now that you are completed with the Code, the two golden Angels thank you for accepting their assistance and leave. We, the Angelic Mothers, gather again around you, thanking you for having the courage to come forth and open your heart again to love and compassion. We now bring you back into your own sacred space. We invite you to take a few deep breaths to come back into your body fully at this point.

We give thanks for all that has been cleared and activated here today.

You are loved and honoured.

We are the Angelic Mothers.

OPENING THE HEART TO LOVE & COMPASSION

Nicole Kishalah 2020

OM MANE UM (22X)

CHAPTER 6

The Ballet of Change

Procrastination: Hesitation to Commit Again

There comes a point in life when we know for sure we need a change. Sometimes it's a little change, and other times it is a major change. We can feel it in our body, our mind, and in our heart. Change means making space for something new, letting go of something, and that something most of the time is not only physical, but emotional. Letting go of old habits, old friends, even old thought forms, is part of the journey. It happens that the fear of letting go makes us hesitate to make changes, and when it comes to hurtful relationships or events, it is very difficult to just take that leap of faith and jump into the unknown of life, so we procrastinate. That procrastination is the hesitation to commit again by your fear to be hurt once more. It is said that it is a natural thing to fear those changes only because we are moving into something that we know nothing about, or not much of.

So we prefer to stay in the old ways simply because we already know its ups and downs, and we have learned to deal with it. As for the new habits we want to create, we have to learn all about them, and that is scary for many, and it surely was for me. But sometimes there comes a day when either you stay in that known space and continue to feel uncomfortable, or you take that leap of faith and go for it.

The Dawn of Change: Changes Taking Place Within

When the Dawn of Change appears, we can feel it deep within us, and for change to happen, we have to open our hearts. There is no other way because we start feeling a little tight in our body, just like a child who outgrows its clothes. For us it's a cloak of life to remove. I remember when I started to feel the need to change in my own life, it became clear I had to start changing from within first. It always happens the same way. First, I have a change of heart, which I can feel deep within me at the beginning. It is like a small spark of light that is igniting deep down into my heart. Once that has taken place and that light shines brightly enough, a mindset change occurs and, gently, the energy of that little light illuminates my mind with this new idea or change that is to take place. I usually give myself time for that process to happen with ease and grace because I do not want to go back to my old ways. Once the idea and energy of the change has taken place in my heart and mind, I can feel it into my entire body, and I take action. Things always seem to go a lot smoother that way.

Living In (Reintegrating) The Body Again

I remember after a life-threatening situation following a surgery and even after the burnouts, I had to choose to live in my body. I chose to reintegrate into my body fully, not halfway or just a little bit; my choice was fully. Even after traumatic events, we often feel that we are not in our body, and most of the time we realize this after the fact, once the turmoil is over. Then again, sometimes we don't. Again, it is a choice we make to live fully in the physical. At times, it was difficult because I knew my body was in pain or I was emotionally suffering. This was not a fun place to be, but deep down I knew I had to make that choice to be able to make the changes in my life. Accepting to be in my physical body meant accepting the beginning of the changes to come and discovering myself, or new facets of myself, throughout the process of reintegrating my body.

Reinventing Yourself After Freeing
Yourself, After Reconnecting to Yourself

Once I started to reconnect to my physical body, I started to reconnect to my soul, my multidimensional being. What I mean by that is all the parts of me throughout all space and dimensions were reconnecting through my heart. I had to learn to accept that there was more to me than just what I could see in the mirror. There was a huge transformation that had started to happen, and I had to reinvent myself, especially since I was always there for everyone else, I had forgotten my own needs and well-being.

To reinvent ourselves after reconnecting to ourselves is a natural process to come to. I mean, if we let go of many thought-forms or old ways that did not serve us for our greatest good, then we have to create some new ones aligned with our heart and new way of being. We need to create something new that resonates at the same level as our new energy, our new frequency.

Self-Respect

This new well-being begins with self-respect. Oh my! Did I ever forget that during the difficult times! I even forgot to take care of myself in the good times while giving a hand to others. Self-respect in itself is a huge step in the right direction of consistent and permanent changes. We set new boundaries with others. At first, I felt mean to do that or feared people would not love me or accept me anymore, and it did happen, but because I started to respect myself, I became more and more peaceful within. This is when I started to realize and say that in life if you do not take your place, others will willingly take yours along with theirs, so why allow that? It was the people who were not happy that I needed to stand my ground with in order to respect myself.

These people were unhappy about the way I was changing because they did not have both their space and my space anymore, only theirs. In the past, since I was not taking mine, they were willingly taking mine also. It was not intentional most of the time for me to let them take my space; it was simply my old pattern. It is just like when there is only one cookie left for two people and one says, *Well, if you're not having it, I will,* and they just eat the cookie because you were not saying anything. It is the same with self-respect. For others to know where our boundaries are, we have to set them clearly with love.

Self-Confidence And Trusting Others

As we get better at setting our boundaries and expressing our needs clearly, we can begin to see the changes taking place in our life and also how our self-confidence is on the rise. Self-confidence is a very important step because until I had enough self-confidence, I couldn't trust others. It was only when I had gained my self-confidence back that I was able to begin to trust others. I went on a slow pace at first, and I was able to trust only a selected few. It was always an issue for me because each time I had fully trusted someone I was betrayed by them in one way or another, and that was difficult to overcome, but I did slowly make progress.

I made some attempts at trusting people, and when I felt these people were honest and respected me, mostly because I was respecting myself, I would open up a little more with them each time. You know, playing it safe. Trusting others was another great way for me to become more assertive in setting my boundaries and respecting myself. To trust even more, something else had to happen within me.

Transforming Your Thought-Forms, Your Beliefs

Even with all this work I had done on myself, for myself, I felt I had to go further on my quest. For the changes to become permanent and my life to be more fulfilling, I had to change the way I was thinking about my life, about others, about how situations interlink. The way I was thinking was perfect for my old self but now, not so much. My old thoughts would bring me back to the old space I was in, and I did not want that anymore, and I sure didn't want to play yo-yo with my emotions and my well-being.

So, little by little and with many beautiful reads of channeled messages and books, I started to have a new outlook on life. Meditation has helped me a lot on this with the clearing of old thought-forms and also by helping me hold the vision of the best outcome for all. If it was not through meditation, it was through my prayers; I was always asking for the best outcome and for the highest good of all involved. That little sentence transformed my way of creating my own life: *always asking for the highest good of all*. It did not feel selfish as a prayer. Also, who am I to know what is best for others? It is tough enough to know for myself; forget others! So this helped me to accept what is and helped me open my heart wide to receive the best outcome. I was changing my vision, changing my glasses for a clearer model, a model adapted to my new life, my new self.

The Guest: Inviting Your Divine Presence to Take Its Rightful Place

Although I always spoke to God, the Angels, Archangels, and other Beings of Light as if they were my best friends, and to my soul, too, I was not always conscious of my Divine Presence. Yes, that divine part of us that lives deep within our hearts. Many say it, even I have said it, that we are divine; only I had not consciously noticed my Divine Presence and worked with it. I was brought on a new path of discovery by connecting with my Divine Presence. So many times I said it is not for us to go up in the heavens, but for us to bring that heavenly energy into our daily life. Bringing the divine into our actions, into our words, yes, but now I was doing deeper work by being connected to my Divine Presence and learning to work with my Divine Presence. In other words, I invited my Divine Presence to take its rightful place into my heart and in my life—consciously.

Curiosity, a Compass That Leads to New Horizons

I have always been curious. As far as I can remember, I wanted to know about things, especially the physical body. As a young child, before I could read, I would sit down with the medical encyclopedia and look at all the images. It was the same thing for the dictionary. It was my favourite pastime. This was way before the internet. I did not become a doctor. I wanted to be a nurse, but that did not happen either. Instead, I was a natural caregiver and assisted the dying for a few years. So, in the end, the knowledge served me just the same as if I had become a nurse because I was not afraid of what I was seeing. I knew that many types of illnesses or conditions existed. I had seen some pictures of those possibilities in books or read about them later in life or even watched them in some medical videos.

It's always a good thing to be curious and want to learn new things. It opens us up to new possibilities, plus we gain knowledge. What this knowledge did mostly was open up some new horizons for me. I read many spiritual books such as *A.A. Michael* channeled by Ronna Vezane, *Kryon* channeled by Lee Carroll, Joseph Murphy, and many others. These brought me much comfort and helped me to go on new paths and understand more of who I am through love.

The Outlook on Life: Looking at Life In A New Way, In Full Awareness

By applying many of the concepts given in the books I have read, I deepened my outlook on life. I had a new way to look at life and many opportunities to experience these concepts in my life too. I was coming to a deeper understanding of life. I was starting to look at life in full awareness with my God Presence. I was always asking God to guide me on my path, in my day, in everything I was doing. I was beginning to grasp that there was something bigger than life itself and I could feel it in my body, my soul and in my life.

The more I opened to receive the Divine in my life, the more it was apparent. Even if some days I forgot or got angry, I knew God was there for me, but now I was fully aware of it and started to live with this knowledge. Knowing I was guided helped me a lot while accompanying the dying and mostly while accompanying my parents and my in-laws. I knew deep down I was being guided by the Divine when I was with them, and I felt supported and safe.

Grace And Harmony in The Complete Sweetness of Change

Life is made of changes, ups and downs, twists and turns. My life was not a merry-go-round; mine was more of a roller coaster at times, and all the peaks and falls were all worth it. At times, I had to adapt to changes even if I was reluctant to change. I came to realize that the more I resisted the change, the more I felt the pain resistance caused. This is when I used the *Star Trek* Borg's saying: *Resistance is futile,* because like it or not, some changes will happen; that's life, and if we resist it, it hurts even more. If you open yourself to the change and ask to be guided in the changes so they can be done with ease and grace, you will be assisted in the complete sweetness of change.

Meditation

Finding Your Balance
Through Change

Beloved One, as you go through change along your life path, it is important for you to stay in balance in your energies and your bodily system. Not only in your chakras but also in all your bodies. We are the masters Hilarion, Archangel Sandalphon and Mary Magdelene coming forth to you today to assist you through this meditation to find your balance through change, for you to keep a balanced body and mind, which will help you greatly in moving faster and more steadily through this process. We are here to assist you find your own rhythm and balance through change. At times it can be small changes, other times bigger ones; nevertheless, this meditation and Code will assist you greatly in any given situation of change. We are honoured to be of service to you this day. We bless and honour you.

We move closer to you in your sacred space now and invite you to breathe deeply and receive the love-energy that we are sending through your heart now. This love will assist you to raise your frequency and elevate you into a beautiful chamber of love. In this temple of love, you are invited to take place on a beautiful crystal bed where a refreshing violet flame is blazing underneath and all around this table.

Your Guardian Angels are with you now, assisting with the calibration of your energies. Breathe deeply to relax your entire body and your mind now; we are helping you be in complete surrender to the energy of love. Master Hilarion stands to your left and Mary Magdalene on your right, with Archangel Sandalphon at your feet. Divine Mother comes now and stands at your head.

As your Guardian Angels calibrate your energy, we begin recalibrating your bodies. We begin with your emotional body, clearing all energies of overwhelm and emotions that are no longer of service to you and that have created imbalances in your emotional body, thus creating disharmony of some sort with other bodies. Simply put, they are out of sync.

We call forth now the rays of Divine Love, Divine Truth, and Divine Bliss to pour forth into your emotional body now, and you begin to feel relaxed, calmer. Breathe into these rays so they permeate your emotional body entirely.

We begin to work with your mental body now, assisting you to release all tensions and resistances to change. We now clear these energies and call forth for the universal laws of divinity, ease, and grace for you. Receive these energies that will bring more flexibility to your mind and body, extricating you from the rigid energies, thought-forms, and patterns learned as a child in this lifetime so you can give yourself permission to move through change with ease and grace. We ask that you acknowledge that change can be fun, joyful, and easy.

As you receive the energies of the universal laws from your heart, invite these energies to flow through all your bodies now. You receive on many levels at this time; simply breathe and know that we are with you, holding you and assisting you through all this process.

We now move to your physical body, assisting it to release all traumas that may have created blocks to change or created imbalances in your body so you can now navigate your way through change gracefully. We invite you to let go of all the images that you are receiving now. Allow us to take those and put them in the violet flame here around the table. All is being transmuted for your highest good and the highest good of your physical body.

If at any time you feel some discomfort, we invite you to breathe deeply into it to release it with more ease. Whatever happened is all perfect in the divine plan, and you are held and loved. Give yourself permission to release all of this, to free yourself from what has been holding you back from embracing change with all your heart.

As you continue breathing gently, we move our attention to your spiritual body, assisting you to release all old beliefs, restrictive beliefs about change that may come from this lifetime or other lifetimes. Beautiful rays of love, peace, and harmony flow through this body now. Enveloping each belief into a bubble of love, which helps you to release those with more ease and grace. You begin to feel the peace within your heart. We are helping you to release the fear of change and to bring more balance. These rays continue flowing into all your bodies now. Take the time to receive those into each of your bodies now. This will help in the recalibration of each body, and the re-harmonization of all your bodies together.

Continue receiving for the next five minutes of your time. This is an important step at this point as it prepares you to receive the Code, which will complete the clearing in each body and chakra so you can find your balance through change and be able to come back to centre much quicker with grace and ease. We have recalibrated all your bodies and re-harmonized them together also.

You can now look into the **Code:** *Finding Your Balance Through Change*. Intend for it to enter your brow chakra. As you begin to sing its mantra twenty-two times (22X), it starts spinning and goes into each of your twelve chakras, emanating into each of your bodies, lifting up your energy, and the veils of fear of change, which brings more clarity for you and assists you to stay in balance in your heart centre. This Code will assist you anytime you need to recalibrate your bodily system and chakras through change.

Once you are done singing the mantra, we seal the work that has been done and give thanks for you having the courage to step forth this day and embrace the truth of balance through change.

We love you and honour you. Blessed be beautiful soul.

The Enlightened Masters Hilarion, Archangel Sandalphon and Mary Magdelene.

FINDING YOUR BALANCE
THROUGH CHANGE

Nicole Kishalah 2020

KOA RAKI ODO NAMA (22X)

CHAPTER 7

The Country of Peace

The Arrival

When you travel to a foreign country, upon your arrival, you need to adapt to their way of living in this new country. Add to that the difference in language, the difference of temperatures, etc.; it means you lose your points of reference. All your senses become alerted, and your brain keeps trying to analyze and make sense of what is going on. It felt similar to me as adapting to live in peace from within was quite different than what I had anticipated. Like everyone else, I had my idealistic, almost romanced image of living in peace. What I did not foresee was how I would react because now no triggers were being activated. My body, my mind, and my soul were becoming one as peace was settling in my heart. Alignment to my true self was about to begin as I entered my own Country of Peace.

Visiting

I did explore by reading about different ways to live in peace. I even took the time to look at how others were living peacefully, only to realize it all began from inside me. But how to begin to live in peace, to be at peace within? As you can see, I was still in my *hurry-mode* to accomplish things, but I could not rush peace. There are certain things in life that you cannot rush, and peace is one of them. So, I started visiting my own heart again to see where peace was needed. I began encountering all these different parts of me that desperately needed peace so I could release these blocks or wounds and be able to move beyond the pain and suffering lodged within me—so I could embark on my life's journey peacefully and discover where my spiritual path was leading me.

The Path of Forgiveness

The first thing that needed to be done was forgiveness. Hopping onto this path was quite a commitment to myself because not only did I have to forgive what others had done or said to me, I also had to forgive myself for not only what I did to others, but also what I refused to recognize within me. I had to forgive myself for what I did not do, what I reacted to, or when I did not react in different situations. You know these reactions are described in psychology as the Fight, Flight, or Freeze response.

It wasn't life happening to me. It was me living my life with all I know and having to connect to what was so deeply engraved in my heart that no longer served me in any way, shape, or form. I had to look at all that baggage that I was carrying along for no reason and that I could easily release. When I did this, I would feel lighter, and the path of forgiveness became an easier path to walk upon, a path where I made amazing discoveries about myself and became conscious not only of what I was releasing but also what I was accepting in my life.

The Choice

Once on the path of forgiveness, you are faced with choice—yes, that liberty of choice that we are born with. But sometimes choosing is not what we want to be doing. As you remember, I was so good at giving my power away that I allowed others to choose for me, but I could not do that anymore if I wanted things to change profoundly in me. I do remember sometimes telling God that it would be easier if I received the answer of what I had to do. But you and I know that this would defeat the entire experience of liberty of choice.

As much as I hated when others chose for me, there were times where I wished they did. That was my head thinking, not my heart, because deep down, I knew I wanted to be in my power. Slowly, and with much respect for myself, I started to make new choices, at times with ease, and other times very timidly. I gave myself permission to choose instead of saying I was making mistakes. I would allow myself to change my mind or make a new choice if the first choice did not work out for me. The choices had to come from a place of self-respect entirely for me to be able to create the change that was coming. Also, I needed to allow the space needed for those changes to occur and bring me closer to my authentic self.

The Authenticity of Self: The Hidden Pearl of Your Heart

The more you clear the old stuff and forgive yourself, the clearer you become about who you are and of your worth, and you become at peace within. Once I was at peace within my heart, I was able to connect to what is the most precious part of me, my authenticity. This was a wonderful moment to be able to sit in my peaceful heart and connect to my true self and discover who I really am. Not according to So-and-So, but according to *my* authenticity, *my* divinity.

Those were precious moments of deep and clear intimacy with my Being. I was able to receive all the love I needed to see me through all that was coming my way and be at peace with it. Connecting to my heart became much easier to do, and I was able to discover more about my Divine Self each time, by connecting to my soul and accessing all the divine wisdom of my heart. Becoming true to myself and my authentic self, being able to express it and not being afraid to show my true self to others, hypersensitivity and all, made me feel truthfully alive. It was liberating to allow myself to be ME, and it made it possible for me to live with an open heart a lot more every day.

Sincerity

Once I connected to my heart, I had to recognize all that was there— my stories, patterns, or even thought-forms—were part of who I am. I had to be sincere with myself and not judge myself for having those as part of me. After all, they made me who I am, but it was not necessary to carry these with me anymore. Being sincere to oneself was said to be something like being true to yourself. But for me, I see a difference. You can be true to yourself, meaning that you do or don't do something out of respect for yourself. But being sincere with yourself has a much deeper meaning. There is no judgment in that space. Sincerity does not judge; it simply shows what is there, puts it into light so you can look at it and love it no matter what. Looking equally at the bad and ugly as much as the good and beautiful and still being at peace in your heart is my understanding of sincerity.

Connection to: Self, Earth, Heavens, The Divine

The more you are at peace in your heart, the more you are able to have a deeper connection to your true self, the Earth, the heavens and to the Divine. We can use different ways for our deep connections. All that is needed is an open heart, a pure intention, and giving yourself permission for this connection to be.

Connecting the sacred flames of the heart to the Earth brings great support for the physical body and the mind. It helps to ground your energy to the Earth and feel the stability it brings and feel more at peace. Focus your attention through your heart to the Earth's heart and breathe into the energy that the Earth is pouring to you.

Connecting to Source brings forth all the Divine Energies that you need in that moment to elevate your frequency and receive divine wisdom through your heart and anchor it to the Earth. For a deep connection to self, rest in your heart and allow the energy to flow freely through your heart to all your chakras and receive the wisdom of your heart from that space.

Your connection to the Divine is done by expanding your heart and also by connecting to the energy field around you. Through your breath, you receive and expand the energies and stay attentive to the messages that are coming for you.

I use the breath a lot to help me receive and anchor energies and to help me realign and re-centre myself throughout the day. I simply take three deep breaths and I am there, back into my heart centre, connected to the Divine.

Connecting to Source brings forth all the Divine Energies that you need in that moment to elevate your frequency and receive divine wisdom through your heart and anchor it to the Earth. For a deep connection to self, rest in your heart and allow the energy to flow freely through your heart to all your chakras and receive the wisdom of your heart from that space.

The Sacred Bonds

Throughout the years, I have communicated my agreements, or disagreements, to my Guides and Beings of Light that I felt present with me. I used to say that it's not me gaining medals in this life; it is my Guides because I am stubborn. They have been immensely patient with me, always guiding me lovingly. It's easier for them as they have no judgment. Once I started to connect deeply to my divinity, I started to connect to other Beings of Light, ones that I did not know of and who were entirely new to me. Some did accompany me for quite some time, others only for a short period, until I understood the lesson of the moment. Others come and go as needed on my path.

Those sacred bonds are not limiting nor limited; on the contrary, they are uplifting, loving, and very respectful. They reminded me many times of the liberty of choice I have and also that there are many possibilities for me to choose from and no wrong or right choices. I was learning to live and to experience life in another way, a very different way than what I had done so far in my life.

These sacred bonds have been the constant help throughout my life and always will be. As they have become stronger and deeper, they have held me in the most difficult times even if I did not feel it. I did not need to feel them present; I knew they were there for me holding the space, the energy, holding me until I was back on my feet again and ready to move forward.

Saying Yes to Life! To The Discrete
Signs of Life. Letting Yourself Be Guided

Although I have been a clear-sentient all my life and an empath, I did not always accept this part of me. But at this point in my life, I was ready to say YES to life again and be aware of what was going on in my life and within me. I slowly became more aware of the subtle signs of guidance. I started by being aware of the little things that did not impact my life in any major way.

For example, asking my Guides which color of clothes I should wear for the day that would bring the best energies for me throughout the day. Or buying a book because I felt the nudge to buy it, and later coming home, and someone would be talking about that specific book, and I would offer it to them. It could be as simple as walking into a bookstore, going within my heart, and asking to be guided to the perfect book for me. There would be a book in particular that my eyes were attracted to, and I would pick it up, read the back of it, and it was exactly what I needed in that moment in my life, in perfect alignment with my path.

There were also the times where I would think of a specific friend and felt I needed to call her. As soon as she answered, she would say, *Oh! I'm so happy you called. I needed to talk to you.* Another time I was inspired to send a paragraph of a book that talked about forgiveness to someone I know. A few months later, I learned that when this person received that message, it was exactly at a time where this person was having difficulty with self-forgiveness.

The one that had the most impact on me was when I suggested to my mother to come with me for a vacation to visit her sisters. She refused at first because it was far, 490 km away from where we lived, but I insisted and told her: *Mom, I don't know why, but I have to take you. It is insisting that we go. I can feel it in my gut, and it is so strong. I have never felt anything this strong before.*

So, we went. It was in the month of July. She visited her two sisters and later visited her brother, who had Alzheimer's disease. Everyone who knew him told her not to go because he doesn't recognize anyone anymore. My mother decided that since we had come all this way, she would go. As we visited with him, my mother asked him, *Do you recognize me?* He replied, *Of course I do, Margot.* We were all teary-eyed and deeply touched.

Two months later, September, one sister died unexpectedly, and three months after her death, in December, her other sister died. You can imagine how surprised I was when my mother called me to thank me for insisting to bring her to visit her sisters and brother. Each time I had a confirmation I would celebrate it by acknowledging, recognizing I had followed my intuition intentionally. I would say, *Yes, I did it!* or *I was right to follow my intuition.* I became more and more conscious and aware of all the little signs around me and tried my best to follow them as often as possible.

It was my way of saying *yes* to life again, but this time a mindful *yes.* I was living my life in a mindful way while knowing there was always room for the Divine in me to be expressed more.

That became clearer after the surgery that had been scheduled a few months earlier. The day of the surgery, while waiting to go into the operating room, the nurse asked as she looked at the lady next to me, *So Mrs. Thibodeau, you are here for a hysterectomy?* She replied, *NO!* I replied, *I am.* Imagine that! We had the same family name and luckily the nurse asked the question, otherwise who knows what could've happened!

With that settled, as it was time to go into the surgery room, I felt a presence coming over me saying, *No, you cannot go now. It's not the right time.* I replied in my head, *I have no choice; all has been scheduled for months now.* So, as we go in, I see the anesthetist, and I have a bad feeling. I push it all aside. I can't really say, *Listen Doc, I don't feel it's the right moment for me to have an operation right now. Let's wait, shall we?* They would have thought I was crazy, plus you do not just turn around like that when the doctor is all ready.

Without saying a word, I allowed the surgery to go forth. Shortly after the surgery was finished and I was in the recovery room, I woke up to the nurse screaming at me to breathe. I was trying so hard to, but my body was slow to recover from the anesthetics. Once I was moved back into my hospital room, an internal hemorrhaging began. New tests were scheduled, and I was to drink a certain liquid to go for a CT scan, and I had an allergic reaction to it. More meds were administered to counteract the allergy. I was out like a light in no time.

I rarely take any medication, so with that cocktail for pain and the allergy, my sleep was heavy. I was so out of it that I didn't even feel the transition from the bed to the CT scan table. When I finally woke up, I was in it, then again, I was out of it, and I don't remember going back to my room. Later that night, I went back into surgery to stop the bleeding. I was weak but alive.

While the doctors and nurses were doing their best to keep me alive and my dear husband was standing by my side, I was living a very different reality. It became clear to me that if I became nervous, I was not going to help the doctors and it would increase the blood flow and make it worse. (Divine wisdom was talking to me at that moment.) At one point, I saw this intense and beautiful light, I felt at peace, but then I was pushed back to life so quickly. No explanations were given.

There I was, back into my physical body. From there, it was time for me to make the choice to embark on my Divine Life Path and play my role entirely or not. No more sitting on the fence would be allowed. I had to choose to live fully with all my gifts or not. I had to take a position. It did not feel as if I was pressured, but it was time for me to make the BIG choice. I did say *Yes,* and with that, I became clearer about being guided, held, supported, and free to be who I am with the inner gifts I have, that are held in my heart, the gifts that my soul has mastered and that I had yet to discover. My soul and Divine Presence would have a bigger role in my life from then on.

Meditation

Opening Your Heart to Receive More of Your Essence

Beloved, because you are more at peace within your heart, you can now connect more deeply to your essence, and you can have a more conscious connection to your Divine Presence. You have travelled the worlds, the galaxies, and chose once again to incarnate on Earth, this beloved planet that is so special to your heart and your soul. You do feel this special connection when at peace within.

We invite you now to take place in a very comfortable position as long as your spine is in an erect posture if you are sitting down, or straight if you are lying down. We invite you now to feel your body, consciously visiting each part of your body with your inner eyes and your breath. This will help you release all tensions and discomfort for this meditation.

We are the Council of Five; we are coming forth to you once more, and it is with great pleasure that we come to assist you to have a deeper connection to your essence. For you to open your heart even more, so you may receive more of your essence. We bless you and honour you for coming this far on your journey. The journey back home to your heart may at times seem difficult, but we assure you that you are always assisted and guided when you call to us for guidance.

As you bring your attention to your heart centre now, we invite you to release all that is holding you back at this time, all that is preventing you from opening your heart to receive more. The Secret is no secret at all Beloved; it is simply a way of being. Being at peace within helps you to surrender even more to your Guides and to your Council of Five. Trust that you are held in the love-energy that embraces you entirely for you to feel totally safe. As you rest in this loving energy, we begin transmitting energies of love and strength through your heart. We invoke the Universal laws of love, light, karma, forgiveness, joy, and peace to be activated into your heart now so you may release all under these laws with ease and grace.

We invite you now to call in all parts of you that do not trust your Divine Presence to come forth, so they can be held in a love-energy. So they may release the old beliefs, patterns, vows, and contracts of distrust of your Divine Presence. Trust that they are held, and they are brought to a temple of love to receive the healing that is for their highest good and for your highest good. Angelic Mothers welcome them now and embrace them and hold them gently wrapped in their wings of light.

These parts of you feel the gentleness of the Angelic Mothers and surrender to their assistance, and they begin to open their hearts to love and begin to receive the blessings of your Divine Presence. Two Angelic Mothers come forth now to be with you as they embrace you; they wrap their wings of light around you, and you feel as if you melt into their embrace. Allow yourself to surrender entirely to their loving hearts.

They begin now to clear each doorway of your heart of old energies that no longer serve you for your highest good and also clear the beliefs that you are not good enough, strong enough, or intelligent enough to be connected to your essence and to your Divine Presence. We tell you, Beautiful Soul, that you are already perfect for this connection to your Divine Presence and ready to open your heart to receive more of your essence.

We call now for the rays of love, peace, truth, wisdom, and grace to pour forth through your heart as the Angelic Mothers continue clearing the doorways of your heart. As these rays permeate your heart chakra and all the doorways, it begins to clear the connections to your heart. Continue breathing deeply and gently as this process is occurring. You are held by many of us, and the Angelic Mothers begin to clear all ties that no longer serve you of fear of connecting to your Divine Presence, of fear of receiving more of your essence.

They begin now to enhance and purify the bonds of love that set you free to connect to your essence. As you receive this, all parts of you that are in the temple also receive with you. You all work together receiving these energies to clear old belief systems and create new energies and strengthen your trust in your Divine Presence and your heart.

The doorways of the heart and the love connections have been cleared now and upgraded to your new energy level for your highest good.

To continue to open the heart and receive more of your essence—and activate the energies of unconditional love and trust to a higher level of frequency—we invite you to take the **Code:** *Opening the Heart to Receive More of Your Essence* that has been prepared for you with this meditation. Look into it and allow it to enter your brow chakra and go down into your heart chakra.

This process is simple and yet very powerful. As this Code comes into your heart chakra, it starts spinning and begins to release all the encodements, the frequencies that will assist you to open your heart with grace and ease to receive more of your essence. As your heart begins to open, we invite you to start singing the mantra of this Code thirty-three times (33X) in long resonant tones. This allows the vibrations of this mantra to reverberate throughout your entire body and soul, which will also bring your energies into alignment with your heart energy.

Once you are done singing the mantra, sit in silence for a few minutes to receive from your heart more of your essence.

All parts of you have now been healed and have now chosen to return to Source. They thank you for accepting them without judgment and giving them the opportunity to clear and heal their hearts too.

We now seal all the work that has been done.

You may work more than once with this Code as long as you do allow some time in between each session to rebalance your energy for a few days before you do it again. We are honoured to have worked with you this day and to be of assistance to you. We love and honour you. Blessed be, Blessed be, Blessed be.

Your Council of Five.

OPENING THE HEART TO RECEIVE
MORE OF YOUR ESSENCE

Nicole Kishalah 2020

KORO MANI Y (33X)

CHAPTER 8

The Mountain of Joy

The Ascension

I love hiking in the woods and in the mountains. You never know what you will encounter and see, but one thing that is for sure is that we are surrounded by beauty and life. The forest regenerates me deeply. As a child, we lived on a farm, and most of my memories are from playing in the woods. I remember finding a big rock I loved to sit on. It was hard to climb on top, but once there, it was the height of joy and peace.

I can compare my life to a long hike in the woods. At times, there are beautiful rest areas, in other places it is harder to climb, and other times it is so difficult that you think that you won't make it. Then, suddenly, you are at the top of the mountain, and there can be a breathtaking view that brings tears of joy and fills your heart so much that it overflows.

Life to me is similar in the sense of taking the time. Even in the difficult moments, I take time to stop and enjoy the beauty around me. How many expressions do we have that express that? There is "Smell the flowers," "Count your blessings," and mine is "Take a breather."

The ascension to joy is not a linear thing, nor is it all difficult either. The more often I took the time to rest and look at all that was good in my life and made me happy, the more I felt the joy of life in me. At times I had to remind myself of that, remembering that it was not just a destination but a journey I had undertaken and that it can be done with more grace, ease, and joy.

Freeing Yourself from Your Own Chains

To bring in more joy, ease, and grace into my life, I would have to free myself from all the chains I was holding on to. I had put these chains there myself throughout my life. Some of them came from being a perfectionist, others from not giving myself permission to do something to please myself just in case I would hurt someone. I learned to accept doing things in a different way, which meant having more flexibility with others and with myself.

To free myself from my own chains, what did I do? I turned to the Divine, and again I asked for assistance to clear what needed to be cleared and to also understand what was of the highest good for me. As more chains were lifted and cleared, the more I felt liberated from my blocks. I was able to see more clearly where I was going in life, which path was possible for me, and which ones I wanted or did not want to embark on or experience. I had never experienced this new freedom before. I had so many limiting beliefs and thought-forms or patterns at play that once I cleared them, it helped me lift the layers and see the truth hiding beneath all that. Just like a beautiful diamond ready to shine all its beauty.

Discovering Your Truth

Once you connect to this diamond in the rough, you will begin to tap into the deep truths that reflect your true identity. This truth at times was scary for me only because I feared change. *What if I don't like what I find? What if people don't like me anymore?* Those were only small fears in the path of discovering what would become the best version of myself—a happy, truthful version. Each time I chose to stand in my power, I was standing in my truth. And that truth was not to be compared to any other because there was no comparison to be made.

Although we are part of a whole, we each have a different frequency, which makes us unique. This frequency comes from all the lifetimes we have experienced throughout the universe and different planes and here on Earth. These make all the fine and delicate vibrations of our being. By discovering this, I discovered my own freedom. I became free of my own limiting beliefs, free of all ties and obstacles that no longer served me. It made my heart want to sing more and more the joy of living freely and truthfully.

The Magic of Words and Energies

We have all heard this before, *Watch what you say, you will attract this.* It made sense in a way, but I did not fully understand the full meaning of it. It is only when I learned to work with mantras that I discovered how powerful words and sounds can be. I started to use them and felt their frequencies and how the energy they carry is important. *Use your words wisely* now had more depth to it than ever before.

It is only when I learned to work with mantras that I discovered how powerful words and sounds can be. I started to use them and felt their frequencies and how the energy they carry is important. "Use your words wisely" now had more depth to it than ever before.

Of course, choose the words to express something clearly, not using them on the reverse of their meaning like we do when we are being sarcastic. I then started to say, *Use the right words for the right thing.* Simple, right? Well, not always. It was not always something I noticed that I did all the time, but I did pay closer attention to this.

Mantras, on the other hand, would free my mind and bring me to the space where only my body would vibrate to their sound, and healing and clearing would occur. It made opening to my truth, the Divine within me, even more peaceful, more joyful, and easier. It created a space where the mind doesn't need to engage in order to have an understanding of what is going on or to receive what is of the highest good for me at that particular moment. It is a space where healing can occur in the most gentle and simple way.

The Impact of Healing the Heart:
Self, Family, and One's Lineage

I started to heal my body, mind, and soul on so many levels, which brought changes in different aspects of my life. So, the inner healing I was doing had an impact on the outer world of mine. I began chanting more mantras, listening to guided meditations, and breaking vows, contracts, and all that was needed for my soul to free myself. I did some personal healing with my siblings, my family, and even my lineage and that happened in a way I did not always foresee.

Some of my ancestors would just pop up in my meditations to receive with me. So, we did the work together. I started to change my point of view, opening my heart to them, forgiving them, and asking for their forgiveness also. I began standing in my power and taking ownership of my actions, words, thoughts, and projections, recognizing that I too had a part that weighed in the balance.

When working from your heart space, you stop looking for who is at fault; you only want what is of the highest good for all involved, and that clears the energies much faster. I'm not saying you cannot have feelings, only that when you are ready to do the work, this is what happens. The more love that is poured on the situations, the faster the situations will resolve, but always ask for the highest good of all involved. I had gotten to this point of letting go of this huge baggage I had been carrying on around throughout my life. Some days were easier than others, and in the end, more and more peace came into my heart and my life along with more joy.

Back to Activity with Joy

Having more joy meant going back to my activities. I now had a clearer idea of what I wanted and what I did not want any more in my life. This brought some major changes in my choices of activities and work, and I was at peace with that and could foresee that all would be much better from then on.

Having more joy in my heart also meant I was bringing that joy everywhere I went. No matter where I was, who I was with, or what I was doing, I now understood that all that joy came from within me. Those days of looking outside of me to fill my heart were over. I could feel I was filled with love, joy, and peace. All that was already there in me; I only had to reach in to connect to it, to become one with it.

Meditation

Opening Your Heart to Joy

Beloved One, as you noticed as you read, healing of the heart plays a major part in bringing back joy into your life for you to feel lighter and stronger. We are Maytrieya, Ascended Master accompanied by Mary Magdalene and Mary. We come to you as a Trinity today to assist you in healing your heart, mind, and soul of limiting beliefs that prevent you from moving forward and raising your frequency to heal your heart. Along with thought-forms, patterns, and attachments that hold you back from living in your joyful self. Clearing all of these on a personal level, family level, and with your lineage.

As you prepare for this meditation, take a deep breath. A beautiful temple of amethyst crystal is activated, and you are invited to step inside. Breathe this beautiful energy that flows in this temple of healing. All the walls of this temple emanate frequencies that your soul recognizes.

As you enter, we come forth to meet you. Mary Magdalene steps to your left and Mary to your right. They both hold you in their embrace of love and compassion. Lord Maytrieya steps forth in front of you now and blesses you and shares:

Beloved, we are honoured to have you with us this day; you have come a long way to reconnect to your joy which is your birthright. You have felt at times that so many things were in the way of your joy, and we say to you that only your fears, limiting beliefs, and patterns were in the way, blocking your heart to open with joy, and for you to notice that this joy has always been part of you. We understand that at certain times it may have been difficult to connect to it, but it is always part of you.

So today we invite you to call in all your lineage of ten generations back to come and join you in this beautiful temple of healing. Angels and Archangels come to this temple to greet them so they can feel at ease, safe, and loved. Call out to all your lineage to come and receive with you this clearing of the heart and the bodies. You see, some memories have been carried around for lifetimes, centuries too. Carried from one generation to another, belief systems that helped you once but that don't serve you anymore. All those patterns developed in this lifetime or from ancestors that you still carry within you.

We come this day to assist you and your lineage to clear all that blocks you from reaching the joy and living from your joyful heart. We invite you now to call in your family to come and join you and your ancestors here in this temple. They, too, are greeted by Angels and Archangels who will accompany them through this clearing.

As all of you are gathered in a big circle in the temple, a big amethyst flame blazes in the centre of the temple. We invite all of you to now open your heart. This is a safe place for you to open your heart fully; there is no judgment, only love. As you begin to open your heart, Angelic Mothers come to assist you to open your heart even more to release the fears, the beliefs, the thought-forms and the patterns that have been preventing you from opening your heart and connecting to joy. We help you to let go of all that has been holding you back and send all of this into the violet flame in the centre of the Temple.

Angels and Archangels sing to help you, your family, and your ancestors to release all that has held you back and that has been carried down from one generation to another. Continue breathing without judging what comes. Simply allow it to come to the surface to be released now. Continue this exercise for a little while longer now. Trust that all that needs to be released and cleared is releasing and clearing. You are doing great. Once you feel all that is needed to be released has been released, take another deep breath and come step into the violet flame.

As your heart has been cleared, it is now your bodies that will be cleared by the violet flame. This flame is gentle and cool. As you step into it, continue breathing and stay in it for the time you need. We now invite all of your family and ancestors to step into this flame and it gets bigger and expands to envelop all who have gathered here today.

As you are standing in the violet flame, we invite you to take the **Code:** *Opening Your Heart to Joy* that has been created to deeply clear your heart and activate the flame of joy in your heart and expand it.

This Code will assist you on each of these levels: self, family, and with your lineage. As you look into this Code, it enters through the brow chakra and gently goes down into the heart chakra where it begins to spin and activate the energies of clearing and opening the heart to the joy. Then begin to sing the mantra twenty-two times (22X).

Take your time with this process to benefit even more from it. Continue looking at the Code and breathing into it whilst singing the mantra. Amazing transformations will occur within you, and you will begin to feel the joy that lives within your heart. When you feel complete, step out of the violet flame. Give thanks to all your family and ancestors who have come to do this work with you now.

We now bless you, your family, and your ancestors and thank all of you for coming forth today for this healing of the heart and reconnection to your joy, the flame of joy that lives within your heart.

Once you have done this process with this meditation, you will be able to simply call for the violet flame to activate around you. Look into the Code: *Opening Your Heart to Joy* and sing its mantra for the healing journey of the heart of self, family, and lineage to activate the joy of the heart.

We are honoured to have been your assistants for this and give thanks to all the Angels, Archangels, and Angelic Mothers who have come to assist all today.

Blessed be, Blessed be, Blessed be all who opens their hearts to their joy.

OPENING YOUR HEART TO JOY

Nicole Kishalah 2020

CHARI AMA NE UM KARI AMA NE UM (22X)

CHAPTER 9

Arriving Home—Love

Loving Yourself Again

It was all fine and dandy to forgive others and take ownership of all the things I had done, but loving myself without judgment was another thing. First, I had to forgive myself for all that I had become conscious of and taken responsibility for. My intentions were never to hurt anyone. On the contrary, I had been a people-pleaser, making sure all were happy and in harmony, but now it was time for me to love myself. I did not have the faintest idea how to do that at first, and because of my upbringing of always putting others first, I felt so selfish. Also as a Catholic, it was considered a sin.

When I started to understand that I could love myself with all my beauty and flaws, I felt less pressure. Much healing had been done, but what was gone had not always been replaced by love, and now I was ready to do that. After all, I would never be able to love others or allow myself to be loved for who I truly am if I didn't love myself. I learned to be patient with myself also when my inner perfectionist was kicking in, wanting all perfect at the get-go.

I was starting to learn to turn inward even more deeply than before to find that love that existed within, and boy, did I cry when I connected with it. I had never imagined how wonderful it could feel, and to think that it was always there in me while I was so busy looking outside of me to find this love! This also brought some changes in my life, such as the way I perceived events, people, and mostly myself, and it became easier to perceive my inner guidance.

Breathing to Live in Your Body and Your Heart

Because I was connecting more and more to my heart and was able to receive more guidance, one day there were some unexpected emotions coming up. As I tried to repress them, I was gently guided to breathe into them—long deep breaths to connect to the emotions and create that bridge between them and my heart for them to be embraced and let them go. I did not need to know where these came from at that time I received them; just simply breathe into it to free yourself.

This is when I discovered the power of the breath. I breathed to release more and learned to breathe to be in my physical body. The breath gave me this liberty to explore my bodies, my chakras, and to live more consciously in my body. I became aware of where the breath was going and how it would undo knots, ease the stress, release the pain, and most importantly, bring me back to my centre, my heart chakra. Breathing brought me to another level of understanding of myself and my ability to live fully in my body and be in the moment.

At times when I felt stressed or overwhelmed with such a busy day, I would escape to the bathroom. I would lock the door and take a few long and deep breaths just to clear all the energies that were clinging to me. Right away, I would feel the shift and become more at peace and ready to go back to whatever I was doing, fully re-centred. That was the power of my breath.

Freedom Through Self-Love

The more I practised breathing, the more I integrated into my body and connected to that deep, profound energy of my heart. It seemed easier to love others at times rather than loving myself. At first, I had some echoes from the past in my mind saying this was wrong, I was not good enough, I was not lovable, I was a nobody, and nobody noticed me. It is amazing how my mind brought back the memories of what I had heard in my childhood from family or friends. Comments that were repeated many times, and even if they were not directed to me, I took them personally. Also, I just wanted to do good by all.

It was quite a change to finally start opening my heart and gently connecting to it and to the love that was there. I was beginning to really connect to the best part of me that I had longed for, for such a long time. The more I allowed myself to feel that love within me, the faster I was starting to feel stronger and able to set healthier boundaries with others and respect myself. I was beginning to have more self-love and more respect for myself too. I was feeling even more alive. I started to feel free simply because I allowed myself to feel that love that came from the depths of my being, of my heart, and I could feel the expansion of my heart chakra starting and it was wonderful.

To be Lulled by Love

One thing I enjoyed was to sit and receive the love or emotionally bathe in it. Allowing the love to come and infuse my entire body, my mind, and my heart was a blessing. I even sometimes went to bed asking to be held in that love while I slept so I could receive what was the best for me. Also, I asked for me to be able to radiate that love to all I encountered during my day. The Infinite Love that inhabits my heart was holding me at all times, on all occasions, and I felt secure.

Again, at this point I gave myself permission to feel the love that sits in my heart. I was not looking outside for this love nor waiting for someone else to say they love me to feel loved. I was becoming aware of old patterns and limiting beliefs that had been holding me back from loving myself entirely, and I was releasing them.

What Self-Love Brings: Peace, Harmony, Clarity, and Liberty Within Oneself

The more I released the old energies, the old thought-forms and patterns, the more I had room for love to flow through my heart, through my body, and my mind. It helped me to have more clarity on what was really at play in different situations. It also gave me the freedom of not engaging in certain situations. I knew what I was really involved in instead of always trying to fix everything and everyone, many times not succeeding because it did not belong to me or it was not for me to settle that. I was learning to differentiate what I could do from what I could not and to still stay in the love of my heart. From that space, I was able to send love to all who were involved, for them to receive the love if they needed it.

Coming back to self-love is a journey just like a hike in nature. Depending on how willing I was to let go of my old stuff, the journey was easy, intermediate, or difficult, and difficulties arose when I was resisting. Still, to this day you can hear me say, *Resistance is futile; resistance is painful.* It is futile because in the end the more I resisted change, the more painful it was for me to move forward as it simply kept me going in circles.

Love is patient, gentle, and embraces too. Once I managed to let down all the barriers of protection I had put up and fully allow the love to be there and start loving myself, I began to discover new qualities that were there in me. Curiously enough, some of them I had felt as a child, and I was taught not to say that about myself because it was bragging and that was bad. I was slowly reconnecting to this part of me that I felt so many times as a child, the loving, caring, patient child that I was.

That self-love made my heart feel more peaceful and in harmony, I had more clarity and liberty within my heart. I was free to love as I was born to do. What a liberation!

Love, The Lighthouse Guiding You Towards
Your Destination, Your Heart Security

Love in my heart became my lighthouse, my guiding light in life. After healing my heart on so many levels, I began to love myself more than ever, and I was now allowing love to guide me on my personal and spiritual path. I did not always know where I was heading, but I trusted this love, especially that it was taking me on a new adventure of life. I also enjoyed the fact that it was gentle with me. I did not feel rushed nor pressured in anything. I felt respected on all levels,

*Love in my heart became my
lighthouse, my guiding light in life.
After healing my heart on so many levels,
I began to love myself more than ever, and
I was now allowing love to guide me on
my personal and spiritual path. I did not
always know where I was heading, but
I trusted this love, especially that it was
taking me on a new adventure of life.*

and I was thinking, *Maybe I'll have a new job?* However, it did not. Instead, it brought me to my home, my heart, the best place to feel secure at all times.

Arriving home to my heart has brought so much peace within me. I no longer felt lost, alone, unloved, or longing to receive love from others. I was still open to receive this outside love, but I was no longer waiting for it. I wanted to spend more and more time within my heart, my home. So much pressure was off, and I could finally be me, just me, without any pretension whatsoever.

The more I spent time in my heart space, connected to the love-energy and self-love, the deeper my connection to my heart and all the unknown within became. I was starting to wonder how many layers there were in that heart of mine.

Reconnecting to Self, to the Divine, to the Infinite Love of Your Heart

Once I had reconnected to the infinite love of my heart, to self-love, and my truth, I began to connect to the Divine within. That was a new thing for me. Who would have thought I was divine? Certainly not the bullies from school. Not only was I divine, but all people are divine. I was still being guided to follow my heart, and it was guiding me to the most profound part of me, my Divine Presence.

I began to research and learn about it. I began reading everything I could find or taking classes that would help me to go even deeper in my knowledge and discover the truth of my multidimensional being. Divine Mother was a wonderful guide along with Lady Nada. They have held me and encouraged me so much to keep going and become an even better version of myself, allowing me to be the Divine Being in human form.

I was learning to find my balance in this as it was not something we spoke about at home. With their help, I started to follow my inner guidance more, having more faith not only in what was outside of me but also what was always there inside of me. I was trusting more and more my intuition, as I now knew it came from that place of love and I would never want to hurt myself, so I allowed it to show me the way to discover even more about myself.

Divine Love: An Affair of The Feminine and The Masculine
One thing I had never thought about was the feminine and masculine energy. Ha! Me who thought that all men were hurtful. Well, my Divine Presence started to show me that the masculine energy is also love and can also be gentle and caring as much as the feminine energy can, and understanding that, as everyone else, I carried both of them within me.

Oh my! At first it felt as if I was carrying my mother's and father's energies. Soon enough, I began to understand that this was an affair of the Divine Feminine and Divine Masculine, those divine energies, not my parents' energies. That was quite different and then I recognized that all held these energies within them, some consciously, others unconsciously, with some shining brilliantly, emanating it, even embodying it fully.

I learned different ways of consciously connecting to these beautiful energies, receiving from them and working with them. I learned to allow the Divine Feminine and Divine Masculine to uplift me to higher energies and higher consciousness, doing more expansion of my heart and mind and grounding more and more of those energies in my life and on Earth—bringing more healing for my soul and spirit, becoming in unity within and living it in my life.

The Sacred Union Within Oneself

The *sacred union within oneself* was a completely new concept for me, and yet it made complete sense, as if that was the natural thing to do, to be. With the different techniques I learned and applied in my meditations and visualizations, my mind began to grasp the importance of the sacred union within me. It brought me more balance, more stability. It even assisted my relationship with my husband, brought it to another level because now I could see the sacred union within him too, reflecting the beauty of this sacred union of the Divine Feminine and Divine Masculine within, bringing more and more acceptance of these beautiful energies of love and light that co-exist within through which the Divine Feminine and Divine Masculine are expressed.

As this sacred union was strengthening, many parts of me came for healing. These aspects of me, of my soul, were who I was in other lives, other dimensions, not only coming for healing but to be in communion and unity through the one heart of my/our Divine Presence. Each time there is such healing and unity, there is an expansion of the heart and group consciousness that elevates the frequencies of the whole.

By bringing in more energies of love and light, a better understanding of the universal laws and integration of all energies are uplifted and created through this process of reuniting in sacred union. You become an advanced version of a human being; well, actually the version that you are meant to be as per the Divine blueprint of your being.

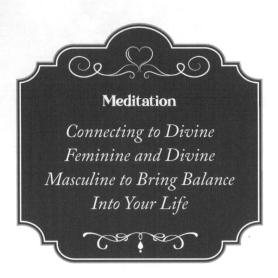

Meditation

Connecting to Divine Feminine and Divine Masculine to Bring Balance Into Your Life

Beloved One, we are Archangel Raphael and Lady Amethyst, and we share with you that to be in unity in your heart, you first have to love yourself, *truly* love yourself unconditionally. We are with you now to assist you to have a deeper connection to your Divine Feminine and Divine Masculine and, thus, have greater balance in your life. At this point, you already know that the breath and your open heart are essential keys for you to move beyond all that holds you back, beyond your fears. And now we ask you to open your heart even more to be able to reconnect to your Divine Feminine and Divine Masculine.

Take a deep breath and release all tensions in your body; allow your mind to relax and let go of any expectations at this point. We call in your Divine Presence to come and oversoul this activation. We also invite two beautiful Angels who stand on each side of you, a beautiful feminine Angelic Being on your left and a beautiful masculine Angelic Being on your right. Their role is to oversee that your energies stay aligned and balanced throughout this activation. Continue to breathe consciously and deeply whilst allowing these Angels to connect their hearts to yours.

Your Divine Presence stands now before you and invites you to stand on a disc of emerald energy. This disc helps your entire being to heal old wounds about the feminine and masculine energies. Give yourself permission now and allow these wounds to be infused by the emerald healing energy. Take your time with this part.

Focus on the love in your heart and allow it to grow and expand. Your Divine Presence blesses all parts of you that also have wounds or fears about the Divine Feminine and Divine Masculine. Your Divine Presence connects to your heart chakra now and pours forth unconditional love, helping you to grow stronger and uplift your faith. It unlocks the truth about your Divine Feminine and Divine Masculine, assisting you to witness the love, peace, and serenity they hold.

The emerald disc now begins to spin and starts going up through each of your chakras. It is clearing all wounds, cords, attachments, fears, beliefs, thought-forms, and patterns that keep you from being in perfect harmony in the Divine Feminine and Divine Masculine energies. It begins spinning in the Earth Star chakra, going upwards Beloved; up into the link chakra . . . up into the base chakra . . . up into the sacral now . . . up into the hara chakra . . . up into the solar plexus chakra. Now as you continue to breathe deeply, allow the disc to clear and heal what no longer serves you. Going up into the heart chakra now . . . up into the thymus chakra . . . up into the throat chakra . . . up into the brow chakra ... up into the crown chakra. Now as it releases higher frequencies, allow your heart to open with more ease and grace to your Divine Feminine and Divine

Masculine. Going up into the soul star chakra now ... keep breathing gently into each chakra as your in-breath brings in all the higher frequencies into the chakras and the out-breath releases old energies. Take a few breaths now as your energies begin to harmonize and your heart begins to open more.

Lady Amethyst comes forth now and puts a beautiful amethyst crystal into your heart chakra and shares with you that this crystal will assist you to trust in your ability to be in harmony with both the Divine Feminine and Divine Masculine energies and be perfectly aligned and balanced in those energies. She invites you to connect now to the Divine Feminine energy of your heart, allow it to speak to you, to whisper into your heart. This Divine Feminine energy of your heart is patient, loving, caring, and helps you in receiving the divine energies through your chakras and your bodies.

As the Divine Feminine energy begins to flow through your heart, allow it to flow through your lower chakras. Going down into the solar plexus chakra ... the hara chakra, filling each one of the chakras with the Divine Feminine energy ... down into the sacral chakra ... into the base chakra now ... into the link chakra now ... into the Earth Star chakra now and back up into your heart chakra and moving up into the thymus chakra now ... up into the throat chakra ... up into the brow chakra ... into the crown chakra ... up into the soul star chakra now and back into the heart chakra, creating an infinity sign of Divine Feminine energy flowing through your chakras, strengthening each chakra and their connections between each of them. As you continue breathing this Divine Feminine energy, it flows with more and more ease, and you feel more and more relaxed and at peace within you.

Archangel Raphael comes forth now and invites you to connect to the Divine Masculine energy of your heart. Give yourself permission to connect to the loving, caring, and energizing Divine Masculine energy. And with your breath now, allow the Divine Masculine energy to flow from your heart chakra to the lower chakras in the same way as you did for the Divine Feminine energy. But this time, breathe in the Divine Masculine energy and allow it to infuse each chakra. Bring it into the solar plexus chakra, the hara, the sacral, the base, the link, and the Earth Star chakra, and let it flow back into your heart, and now up through the upper chakras, the thymus chakra, the throat chakra, the brow chakra, the crown chakra, the soul star chakra, and back into the heart chakra.

Create a new infinity sign, this time with the Divine Masculine energy. Again, take your time with this as with each breath the Divine Masculine energy rebalances each chakra with the Divine Masculine energy, vivifies your chakras and your body.

And now Archangel Raphael, Lady Amethyst, and your Divine Presence infuse your heart with their heart energy to assist you to bring into balance the Divine Feminine and Divine Masculine energies of your heart, which in turn will bring more balance into your life. Archangel Raphael puts a beautiful emerald crystal into your heart to help you to continue to heal what may come and is not in harmony with the Divine Feminine and Divine Masculine energies. This crystal will bring the support you need to keep you in balance in these energies.

As these energies are now in balance within you and you feel harmonized, the two beautiful Angels thank you for allowing them to assist you; and as they leave, your Divine Presence blesses you and your heart and seals the work that has been done today. Your Divine Presence goes with all parts of you who have received healings together with you today and blesses them as they come back to the one heart, back to the unity of the Divine Feminine and Divine Masculine energy into perfect balance.

Beloved One, we are so grateful that you have accepted our help in reconnecting you to the Divine Feminine and Divine Masculine energies of your heart. We now invite you to take the **Code:** *Reunification of the Divine Feminine and Divine Masculine Energies of Your Heart*. Look into it and breathe it in through your brow chakra and allow it to flow into each of your chakras, then sing its mantra twenty-two times (22X). This Code will help you to rebalance your energies through the Divine Feminine and Divine Masculine energies. You are loved, you are held, you are blessed.

We are Archangel Raphael and Lady Amethyst

Blessed be, Blessed be, Blessed be all who chose to live in the balance of the Divine Feminine and Divine Masculine energies.

REUNIFICATION OF THE DIVINE FEMININE & THE DIVINE MASCULINE ENERGIES OF YOUR HEART

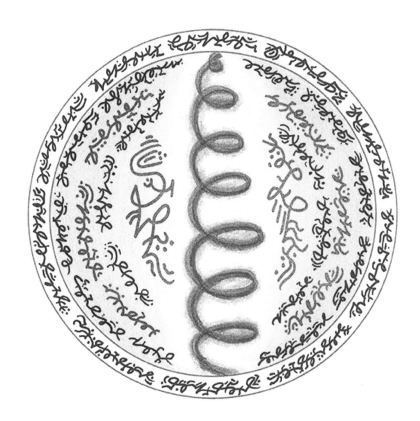

Nicole Kishalah 2020

OMKO ROKI NA TA (22X)

CHAPTER 10

Tools for Life

Alternative Therapies

The day I realized I did not have to do everything alone to bounce back from burnout and other difficult life situations, I began asking where I should turn to. It was not as much my head needing help as my heart wanting to expand for it to release the old, accept the new, and put into action the new things I was learning.

In the beginning, I was so raw emotionally that I refused to talk. I refused to go for any type of therapy. I did not want to talk. I wanted to free myself and felt deeply that talking was not the way to go. So, I tried therapies like rebirth, chanting, reiki, or meditation to liberate the emotions trapped in me, and I tried others to clear my energies. Together with that, I included some acupuncture and massage for my body to feel good.

All of these steps were taken following my intuition, asking for guidance to know where to go next and how to do it. I also asked to be guided to the right person and best therapy for me that would assist me on my journey of healing.

Rebirth was one of the ways I tried first to heal myself, as well as channeling sessions, reiki, clearing my chakras, and attending a group for guided meditations. Those are the type of sessions I had, always connecting to know if we were a good fit to work together and if the energy was flowing clearly. If not, I would look for someone else. After all, I was doing this for my highest good, so I had to feel the connection, otherwise the benefits were not as clear, and it would make it harder for me to surrender to the process.

So, I always respected what I was guided to and how I felt. I wanted ease, grace, and peace in every session. Those are my prerequisites for such deep inner work.

Readings That Inspire

I like to read. So, some of my therapies I found in books, such as *The Cosmic Power Within You* by Joseph Murphy. I found this work early on in my spiritual readings. Later on, I came across the books from Ronna Vezane, who channels Archangel Michael. They were *The Golden Promise* and *Your Sacred Quest*. These books were my recipe books.

So many tools Archangel Michael was giving me; they were quick and easy too, to top it off. It worked fine for me at the time as I was working, married, and had two children. Things have to roll if you want to get somewhere with a young family. Then I discovered Kryon, which appealed to my scientific and practical side, my logic.

It all made sense, and I got so much more from these readings; they brought me to a deeper understanding of what was really occurring within me. Those were the times where I was so thirsty for spirituality I never had enough. Actually, I was awakening.

So, in all, I have read so many spiritual books that the list would be too long to put here. But what is important is that the books that *you* read need to be uplifting, encouraging, and inspiring *to you*, and if they have tools, to use it's a bonus. Also, for me they needed to be easy to read in a simple language and have powerful tools I could use. Remember that at some point, I was still in burnout, so reading needed to be easy as I got tired really quickly.

Discovering Your Inner Toolbox

A few years later, I started to work with *Qala* doing the Grace program, which was called the Christ Emissary at the time. I was discovering different types of tools to continue my healing, I was working with the Divine Feminine for six months, then with the Divine Masculine for another six months, which brought me more balance. Then I learned about light language and Codes (high-frequency, encoded images). Those were so much fun to work with, and they brought amazing results. So, when came time to register for the mystery school of Gaia, I did.

This time, not only would I continue to work with this type of work, but I would also begin to channel. Yes, me who had said, *never in a million years would I allow anyone to use my body to bring a message.* Well, it would appear my soul had chosen something else instead. I knew I was a messenger, but in my mind, it was not channeling. It was simply saying a word or two that would assist someone, or direct me to buy a book, only to find myself giving it away to someone who needed it. That was normal for me.

In that school, I learned how to powerfully ground my energy to channel, how to prepare myself, and how to do the channeling. I continued to discover how to do what I call *soul healings* with the Angelic Mothers. I also discovered the different tools my soul and Divine Presence hold, which I can call forth to assist me in my day or at night, whenever they are needed and not only for healing, but also for receiving and activating different energies to be able to reconnect to my true nature, my divinity.

Love: The Ultimate Tool That Heals from the Inside and Fortifies Us

As I mentioned before, as I healed, I began to understand the real power of love and that it is my most powerful tool to heal, support, embrace, and fortify my connection to my Divine Presence. The unconditional love that our Divine Presences hold is infinite. Love has so many virtues and can be used in many ways. It can also hold the space for all parts of us to come and sit within it to receive its divine qualities.

Another opportunity arose to work with Qala and Amaya, this time, through the Divine University doing the Self-Mastery School of Divine Love course. This course strengthened my connection to the Divine Mother and Angelic Mothers and many other Beings of love and light from other realms.

Strengthening the connection with my Divine Presence and other Beings of Light assisted me to have more confidence in what I do. I was learning how to live with an open heart and allowing the flow of love to permeate all my bodies, assisting me to receive love unconditionally as well as to emanate the love.

Without love I would not have survived, especially without love for myself. At times it seemed much easier to love others than loving myself was. What I came to realize is the more I loved myself, the easier it was to recognize the love in others. I applied love on my own emotional wounds. I called in for assistance at times. If I felt too shaky emotionally, I gave permission to Divine Mother and Lady Nada to help me, for them to bring the love into my life, and to accept that I was love also, not just a broken emotional person.

One important key I learned is each time I cleared something and liberated it, there was a space now available to be filled with by love. The wounds became love, the fears became love, the blocks became love, and the thought patterns became love. And, the more love there was, the more I felt the love from inside and the stronger I felt. I was ready to continue my heart-and-consciousness expansion, and still do.

Crystals: The Silent Friends

When I was young, I loved rocks. I found them magical; I would hold some for hours. To my mother's despair, I tried to collect them. I can still hear her saying, *You and your rocks.* Back then, I felt negated in this connection. Luckily for me, if I could not keep any in the house, our parking lot, which was huge on a farm, was filled with rocks. Some white ones, others with sparkles in them or some green ones, but my favourite of all were the brown ones. I loved their texture, their softness, how they would become warm in the sun and somehow felt different from all the others. To this day, they are still my favourite, I guess they are my childhood love in some sort.

Today I have many crystals. Well, it started with one. I thought it was ridiculous when I heard people saying they talked to their crystals or asked the crystals if they needed something. Now I am that one, and I discovered that inadvertently. One day, during an event where my favourite channeler, Ronna, was in town, she had a table with crystals for sale. There were many people in front of the table trying to find the perfect crystal, holding them in their hands, feeling them, and I stood behind them, asking God to guide me to the best crystal for me.

I felt one strongly connecting to my heart. I looked up at the lady selling them and pointed out one that would not even stand and did not seem very nice to many, and I said, *I want this one.* She wrapped it up for me; meanwhile people are turning around looking at me and saying they wished they could choose one like I did. Well, actually the crystal chose me; God guided me to it. We were a great match for each other.

That night, I put it on my night table before going to bed as I had heard Archangel Michael say that crystals emanate energy that assists you on your spiritual journey. After two hours in bed, I got up to bring the crystal in the kitchen because it was vibrating so strongly, I couldn't sleep at all! And even if it was in the kitchen, from my bed I could still feel the connection to my heart. To this day I still work with this one; it has many friends on my altar now. They are different types and shapes, and some I talk to, listen to, and sing to.

They are my assistants; they can clear energy, they can elevate frequencies, and they can support energies. I simply infuse them with my heart frequency, asking my Divine Presence to attune them to my frequency. Some of them travel with me when needed; others don't like the travelling. It is not their job; they are with me to hold the energy of my space, the house, the family heart. They are wonderful friends, silent friends to work with or simply to connect to.

The Art That Heals, Soothes

Along my journey, I discovered oil painting. At a very young age, I learned how to sew. I could draw okay. I tried different types of arts and crafts, and one day my teenage son asked to have his room painted in a medieval style. Unsure of how to do this, I suggested we paint large bricks, and he said no. He wanted rocks. *How am I supposed to paint rocks?* I wondered.

Knowing that he was better than I at drawing and that I did not have the patience nor the time to draw those rocks, I suggested he drew the rocks for this project. I had found a picture in a magazine that represented in part exactly what he wanted. So, he drew it, and then before I started painting I called my aunt who had been painting for many years. She gave me the most important techniques to get me started and off I went.

As I was halfway finished with a wall my husband came to see how I was doing and said, *If you don't take a painting class, it would be wasting your talent.* And off he went. He had said that in a way that he never did, and it stopped me in my tracks. The next week, as I brought my daughters to their piano lesson, I noticed that there was an exhibition of paintings across the street. One of the paintings caught my eye.

I applied for the class, and even though the teacher said she had a waiting list, I decided to put my name on it. The next day, I received a call to begin the next Monday. I thought that the Universe was saying *it is about time you came for those lessons*. I struggled at the beginning, not understanding the shades, the lights, and other little techniques, and one day, when I had a bad headache, I decided to let go of trying and whatever would be, would be. I was astonished with the result. I realized then that I needed to surrender to the process instead of staying in my head because if I stay in my head, I make mistakes and have to keep starting over.

That brought me to do some intuitive paintings. As a result, a new way of healing for me began, or should I say, my healing process through painting became conscious.

All the arts and crafts I have done in my life have brought me into a space of peace within. It happened simply because my mind would quiet down, I was focused on the task at hand, and time seemed to stop. I was fully present in the moment, so much so that at times I forgot to eat. I feel connected in those moments, entirely connected to my heart and my Divine Presence. That is the magic of oil painting for me.

Try it, even if you feel you are not the best at it. As long as it brings you into a peaceful moment, it is working for you.

Opening Your Wisdom Toolbox, Opening Your Conscience to The Divine

What do I mean by a *wisdom toolbox*? It is all the wisdom that lives in your heart, in your higher mind. With different exercises of meditation and healing modalities, I had learned to open my heart to the Divine within me. It seemed very mysterious in the beginning; after all, it was not something tangible. I heard people talking about how *connected* they were, how it brought them into different states. I was a scaredy-cat, and well, I was afraid of what I could find.

I was afraid of the power I had, afraid to hurt others with my power or my inner gifts. I knew I was a clear sentient, but I did not understand entirely what kind of empath I was. One day, while having an intimate discussion with my soul and my Divine Council, I realized that my Divine Presence would never hurt me because it is me. Simple, right? A new connection in my brain was made, or maybe I should say, a *reconnection*.

From then on, it was much easier to open my heart to my Divine Presence—to surrender to it, to the processes it was taking me through, to clear the pathways of my heart, my journey. It was also easier to accept the new ways of doing the work for myself in a simpler and more effective way. Like I said earlier in this book, *Resistance is futile; resistance is painful*, and I would add, *Surrender is ease*.

Once I learned to ground my energies, to open and expand my heart chakra and my energy field, I began to receive more information for myself and higher frequencies. I gained more assurance. It changed my self-esteem for the better. You, too, can connect to it and embrace it.

Tools To Open the Heart

My personal tools to open my heart are meditation, breathing exercises, chanting, mantras, pure intention of the heart, music, and hugging my cat. Anything that brings you joy helps open your heart to allow the flow of love to circulate and liberate what is not necessary for you to carry anymore.

Meditation

Opening Your Heart
to Your Divine Self

Beautiful One, we come today to meet you on an inner level in your journey back to self-love. We have walked with you on this journey throughout your readings and sat with you during your meditations and supported you whilst activating the Codes that have been shared with you.

We bless and honour you for the journey you have undertaken to come back to the One Heart of your Divine Presence. Each day, you connect more and more deeply to all that is and the divine within you. You can feel the love of your heart expanding gently, and now we will take you on a short journey through a meditation with the crystals to awaken your Divine Wisdom and receive love.

You already know that you are the love that you seek and that we are here to assist you in connecting deeply to this infinite love that lives within your heart space and heart chakra. We are Sananda, Mary, Serapis Bey, Mary Magdelene, and Quan Yin coming to assist you through this meditation. Please take a comfortable position, close your eyes, and give permission to your Divine Presence to come and connect to your heart chakra, your brow chakra, and your base chakra.

By allowing your Divine Presence to do this, you ensure yourself to stay centred during this meditation.

We are Sananda, and we come forth now and bless your heart. We say to you that you are a magnificent being. If you could see how we see you, you would not doubt for a second the beauty of your heart and being. You have walked this Earth many times and keep choosing to come back to experience more and more of the intricacies of duality and also to find your way back to your heart.

We invite you now to call in the energies of the crystals, the beautiful crystals that you may know, or other crystals that come to you. These crystals are now settling around you, creating a beautiful circle. As they are taking their places, you can feel the energies gently shifting. Take the time to notice which crystals are there to assist you today. What colour are they? What shape do they have? What size are they? This simply helps you to connect to the energy of the crystals. These crystals create a temple of love around you now; a field of unconditional love is activated for you to feel entirely secure and safe. These crystals also assist you in keeping your energies grounded whilst receiving and opening your heart to your Divine Presence.

The frequency of the crystals begins to vibrate now and elevate your frequencies. They are powerful and gentle at the same time. As your frequency rises, keep breathing long deep breaths, which help you to open your heart even more and stay grounded. Give yourself permission to let go of all that is holding you back to reconnect with your Divine Self, as therein lies the infinite wisdom of your being and your connection to love. As you give yourself permission for this, you feel yourself going deeper within your heart centre.

Mary Magdelene and Quan Yin come forth now with elixirs of love and trust. They offer you to drink some of it and also pour some into your heart chakra. You begin to feel the transformation happening within your heart now, and with your breath, you give it the space to expand your heart and begin to feel lighter in your heart.

Serapis Bey and Mary come forth now to assist you. As they both stand before you, they bless you and your heart and welcome all parts of you that fear the connection of your heart to your Divine Presence and do not trust your Divine Wisdom. And they invite all parts of you that fear or do not trust to come and receive, in a temple of love, the teachings and the healings that they need at this point. They have come because of your courage to open your heart and because you gave yourself permission to be connected to your Divine Presence. Your courage and divinity will have inspired them to be healed also.

They are now being guided into this temple where Angels come forth to meet them and assist them. As they take their places in this temple, they are shown the beauty of their hearts and of the one heart. They each receive a crystal now for them to put into their hearts, which will assist them in opening their hearts even more to your Divine Presence and divine wisdom.

Send love to these parts of you now, and trust that they are receiving it. As you do this, the crystals around shift in frequency. The more you send love to these parts of you, the greater is the frequency of the crystals. It begins to realign your heart energy to your divine wisdom and divine will. Continue sending love to them as you all heal together now—receive love together.

As the frequency rises, a beautiful vortex activates around you. And in this vortex, you can release all old beliefs, thought-forms, patterns, and ties that have been created throughout the years, any incarnations of distrust in your Divine Presence and divine wisdom.

As you keep sending love, your heart chakra expands. The pathways of your heart are clearing all old energies that no longer serve you in this lifetime, so you can connect deeply to your Divine Presence and tap into your divine wisdom.

You are now releasing all contracts, vows, and agreements you have done across all time, space, and dimensions to not trust or to fear your Divine Presence and your divine wisdom. As you do this, the crystals begin to accelerate the rhythm of the frequency, shattering all of them, and they now dissolve into the frequency of love. As these are clearing, continue sending out love to all parts of you, and they, too, begin to send love to you. You all begin to receive from each other, which enhances the vibration of your heart and assists you to connect to the heart of your Divine Presence more deeply.

As all that is needed to be cleared is cleared, the vortex subsides gently. The crystals around you adjust the frequencies of your body and your chakras. The crystals begin now to vibrate with the love frequency attuning to your heart, as well as to your Divine Presence's heart, to assist you to receive more Divine Love and Divine Wisdom. Open yourself to receive without judgment. Your heart holds all the answers you are seeking in life. You are the answer to your prayers, to what you seek. You are divine and divinely loved. You are the love, you are the light, you are all that you are.

To assist you in connecting even more to your divine wisdom and to receive more love you can now take the **Code:** *Opening Your Heart to Your Divine Self,* which was created to assist you to open your heart to your Divine Self. Look into it, intend for it to enter through your brow chakra and into your heart. As you sing the mantra twenty-two times (22X), it will move from one chakra to another to release old energies and fortify the connections of love between each chakra.

Once you are done singing the mantra, take three deep breaths and give thanks to all parts of you that have come forth to receive with you today. Give thanks to all the crystals that assisted you as they are your silent friends and to your Divine Presence for holding you during this meditation and activation.

We are Sananda, Mary, Serapis Bey, Mary-Magdalene, and Quan Yin; we bless you and seal this work that has been done in this sacred space. You begin now to come back into your own sacred space as you breathe deeply into your body and begin to move your legs and hands gently. It is important for you to give yourself some quiet time after this meditation as you are now in sacred union with your divine heart.

Blessed be, Blessed be, Blessed be dear one.

OPENING THE HEART TO YOUR DIVINE SELF

Nicole Kishalah 2020

AM CHE KARE TA NOME (22X)

CHAPTER 11

The Spiritual Path

Discussing with the Divine: My Best Friend Since Day One

You would not believe how many discussions I had with my Guardian Angel, my Spiritual Guides, my Divine Council, and other Beings of Light. As far as I can remember, I have talked to them just like I can talk to you if you were standing in front of me. I feel like I have been talking directly to you through this book. It is the same way with my Guides. They know everything, and I know I can't hide anything from them. I have even asked them to help me many times by saying, *You know me better than I know myself. Could you guide me, please; give me an insight?*

I recall at a very young age asking them why they had abandoned me here all alone. I felt lonely even though we were a big family. A huge piece of me was missing, and for many years I searched for it unsuccessfully.

I had all kinds of discussions with them and there may have been some awkward moments, but I took the time when I had it. Any quiet moment was always a good moment to have a discussion with my best friends. They were the only friends I knew who wouldn't betray me, and at times I reminded them that I was the one with both feet on the planet and that things might be different in this reality.

My most favourite moment to have a discussion with them was when I was doing a repetitive task, like washing dishes. Those moments are a blessing for me. It is an active meditation; I am fully present, fully connected, and opened to receive their wisdom, their advice, their guidance.

My Mentors

Other than the Angels, Archangels, my Guides, and many more Beings of Light, there were these people to whom I felt a deep connection. There were also the ones who made me look inside me to see what was triggered, where I was hurt and needed the healing. We call those teachers. They are teachers only because they show you the way to the healing needed, the liberation needed. It can be anyone you know, and at times, even a stranger will bring you a message or a lesson.

My mentors through my journey of spiritual awakening have been mostly authors who are channelers and others who had created programs you could work through. More mentors will come on my path as I keep evolving throughout my life, taking me from where I am to the next level. Life is in constant movement; nothing sits still for very long, not in my life anyway.

When The Divine Guides You: Displeased at Times and Enchanted at Other Times

I always discussed with my Guides as if they were my equals; I sometimes objected to what was offered to me as a solution or the loving guidance that was offered. Sometimes my mind was set on one objective or outcome; I was limiting my possibilities. They never argued, though. They let me do what I wanted because they have to respect the Universal Law of Liberty of Choice.

To picture the way I communicate with my Guides, imagine yourself with your best friend who knows you so well and can tell when you are bulls**ting them— they will tell you. There are no filters, and you say things like they are. Well, that is the way I communicate with my Guides; they are my equals. They are so patient and loving with me.

They have guided me through thick and thin. They are always ready to assist me as long as I ask for their assistance. It took a while before I realized that I was asking, but I was not always giving them permission to act on my behalf. I was not allowing them to bring me where I needed to be in a specific moment for my highest good. I asked but I did not allow them to give.

When I began to give them permission and surrendered entirely to their beautiful energy and work, I was letting go of my attachment to the results. Expectations can bring deceptions. The way my mother used to explain this to me was: *You give your problems to God, but you keep holding on to it. What good can come out of this? Either you let Him do His work or you do it on your own. What do you choose?*

I have been guided to do so many things that I had never imagined or that I was sure that I would never do in my life. My mind said *no* categorically, but I followed my heart. Why I followed my heart is simple. I was always positive that God knew me better than I knew myself. Therefore, what was presented to me was always a better option, even the ones that scared me so much, like channeling.

All that was needed of me was to open my heart even more to allow the energies needed for the changes or activations to happen—for my heart and mind to open to the deep love that Mother/Father God has for us all. Transformations occurred, even transcendence.

Becoming The Love Lighthouse

Different physical reactions occurred as I opened my heart to more unconditional love, Divine Love. The most common one was as my heart filled with such love and was overflowing, I would burst into tears. This was only because I was not used to feeling such love. It was something I had never felt in my life before. The deeper I went into the process, the more love I felt until my body finally accepted this love as a natural and safe feeling. The other reaction was that I felt my heart wasn't big enough to hold so much love. I felt as if it would explode, if you know what I mean. Now I know that this feeling was the expansion of my heart, as simple as that.

I learned to carry this love, to emanate it, and wherever I was going to expand it for all to receive. This love holds all divine qualities that benefit all, and, of course, I always asked for the highest good of all. The more conscious I became of the love in my heart, the more I felt it flow through me, and I saw the impact it had on me and on others. It helped me to heal, surrender, forgive myself and others, expand, be of service to others, and so much more.

One day, I received one of the most representative and meaningful gifts from one of my sisters. It was a small lighthouse with crystals to represent the light. She said to me, *This represents you perfectly; you are the love lighthouse that guides people.* I realized that even if it seemed that I was not doing anything, I was always there, well-anchored and shining my light and giving love to others. I felt so honoured and shy when she gave me that. So often I felt like the pillar of my family, husband and children, and there it was, right in front of me, this tiny golden lighthouse with its crystals. My sister added, *You do know that no matter the storm, the lighthouse still shines its light to guide others.* I was deeply touched.

As I continued to learn on my evolutionary path of spirituality, I discovered new Beings of Light and worked with many others. They have held me and helped me open my heart with more grace and ease as much as possible. Luckily, I was also learning not to resist as much as I did in the beginning. These loving Beings of Light have assisted others through me, either by giving a message or prompting me into doing something special for someone without even thinking about it; it simply happened. I was becoming the beacon of light my soul is, thanks to all the divine assistance.

New Divine Connections

When I started the Christ Emissary program, I began to create new connections with Beings I didn't even know existed. I learned how to recognize their frequency when they came into my energy field, close to me. I learned how to communicate with them and mostly learned to ask for assistance from them. Some of them used to bring these beautiful fragrances. In the beginning, I was searching in the house where this beautiful scent came from until a friend told me it was a way for them to signal their presence around me. It was a new way for me to recognize them and instantly open my heart to connect to them and receive the love, the energies that they came to bring me. That, too, was part of my spiritual evolution.

One other sneaky way they had for me to connect with them was through oil painting. One day, my younger daughter, who was so connected to the Archangels, asked for a painting of Archangel Uriel. Because I was still in the beginning stages of learning to paint, I used an image someone else had already created to do so. In fact, the image was simply to help me and my teacher have a clearer idea of what to paint. In reality, I was going to receive the frequencies of this Archangel throughout the entire time I was painting it.

Art took an entire new turn for me, again. Then I painted Quan Yin, again a reproduction of an image. Then, I moved on to Archangel Michael, and with him, my confidence started to rise. As I was getting to the last steps of that painting, I decided, although I was using an image to assist me, to make some changes—changes that resembled what I was feeling and especially how I perceived him.

Instead of pointy rays surrounding him, I put a fluffy type of energy around him with little lights that sparkled. It brought out the softness of the energies I felt from him. When I painted Archangel Raphael, it was quite different. I began with an intuitive background on my canvas. I was simply applying different colours, not knowing what I was going to paint, but asking to be guided for my next painting, and there he was with Mother Mary in the centre. I could feel them in there. Not everybody saw what I could see.

Nonetheless, I stayed connected to my vision and did the entire painting by creating and using all kinds of images to assist me to paint them. Remember, I don't draw that well, so I use all kinds of images to compose a painting, to help have the outline at least. And since then, this is how I create my paintings. I start with an intuitive background and let it speak to me. Or I use what I see in it to create the final look. It is quite enjoyable.

So, through these new Divine Connections, they have used art to connect to me and bring forth the energies and frequencies needed not only for me but for others who see these paintings. And that prepared me to do more artwork.

Divine Mother, Her Love: My Apprenticeship in Channeling and All Her Messages Concerning Love

In 2006, I began my training in the Sacred Mystery School, and this is when I consciously connected to the Divine Mother. It was a deeper connection than I had ever felt. This loving, caring, and supportive energy was wrapped around me and lifted my heart at the same time. I felt it as much within as around me. It was like being held in a cocoon of love. You would think that this would be the love part of my journey, but it wasn't. *Why?* you would ask.

Well, it was only because of my resistance to change; my fears and beliefs of not being worthy, not being good enough, all came to the surface. Another layer was surfacing, but at this point, I had more tools to work with and to help me. Remember earlier in life I had said, *Never in a million years would I let any Being use my body to transmit any messages.* That was the biggest wound yet to heal.

I had cleared thought-forms, patterns, fears, broken agreements, vows, and contracts to help me get through and beyond all this. Divine Mother was always there, holding me in this cocoon of love. There was so much to learn and to let go of, all that stuff I did not need to carry anymore and so much to look forward to and to integrate—giving myself permission to be supported at all times.

I was learning a new side of me, this part that I had always wanted to hide and not accept. This beautiful loving and caring heart of mine connected to the Divine Mother, to our Father/Mother God. I started giving myself permission to be consciously connected and living my divinity on this planet as it was intended from the beginning, but that I had refused so fiercely. With that, I became more and more relaxed, more open.

To help me at the beginning of channeling there were my teachers and some friends, and the one who was oversouling my path was Archangel Faith. That says a lot, doesn't it? I needed to have faith in my ability to channel. I needed her to assist me on that journey if it was only to trust the process and know that I was safe while channeling.

When I began channeling in front of small groups, Divine Mother always spoke of the importance of opening your heart to receive the love. How important it is to give ourselves permission to be loved and allow Her love to pour through all the chakras and through all the bodies and all parts of us, thus bringing us back into alignment, divine alignment.

She talked about how important it is to expand the heart and how love can bring balance in our lives and that it is equally important to receive the love as it is to love others. Actually, all we have to do is to receive the Divine Love and become a vessel of love that emanates the love.

That understanding has helped me to change my own perception on life and of events as my vision was coming from my heart, not only my own eyes and mind. The heart energy was balancing out all energies for better outcomes for all.

One other thing I did was ask to sleep in the heart of the Divine Mother. This assisted me to have a restful night and to receive the teachings I needed, or that were of the highest good for me whilst I slept. Each next morning, I felt well rested and ready to start my day. It was not always the conscious work I was doing; there was as much work done during the night, too, and I loved the fact that I could do this. I had long ago let go of trying to find the answer for everything arising or how to do things. So, this was a beautiful and simple way of doing the work during my sleep as my days were very full already.

The Angelic Mothers and Their Continuous Work with The Souls and Their Infinite Love, Their Compassion

The Angelic Mothers are great healers of the soul; they hold this Divine Mother quality, and when I began working with the Angelic Mothers, I was like a fish in water. As much as I had difficulty in the first nine months of the mystery school, the last three were a breeze. I reconnected to my sisterhood. It was easy to work with them. All the hard work had been done with the Divine Mother, and I was well prepared to work with the Angelic Mothers.

At the beginning, we were practising amongst our group, and one person asked for a session with me; she was in Australia and I was in Canada. We set a time where she would settle in comfortably for her to receive and I would begin on my side. We had no contact by phone or internet during the session. After the session was done, I sent her a little note describing what had been worked on, and she was ecstatic. It was something she had been dealing with for years and was about to meet someone and that meeting was in sync with what was healed with the Angelic Mothers. I was really happy for her and amazed at the work the Angelic Mothers were doing. There was no way I could have known what she needed; all I had was her name.

Once my training was done, I continued offering sessions to people in my area, and some of them would give only their first name because they did not want to lead me into anything. I did not mind because after all the practices I had done, I knew deeply how the Angelic Mothers worked and how potent their healing energy was. Every time people were amazed at the information they received. Some of them had huge transformation in their lives, thanks to the infinite love and compassion of the Angelic Mothers. They know who we are so much so that they can help a person to receive the greatest soul healing and transformation.

I have sat to receive from the Angelic Mothers many times. Each time I call them in, they are there. I also call upon them for anyone who asks for assistance. Since this training, I have been offering soul healing sessions with the Angelic Mothers and done channeling with Divine Mother and other Beings of Light. They are the ones who guided me to write this book so to be able to connect with you in a more personal way.

Here's a small message channeled for you:

Know that you are loved and cherished more than you can ever imagine. Allow the Divine Love to flow through you as a river of gentle, caring change that will bring more flexibility in you. And with that love, you will always have the support that you need to see you through tough times. Your heart will become your safe haven, the place where you can always seek refuge to heal and clear, or simply sit and be in the love. You are always awaited there with great anticipation to reconnect with you. Know that you are safe and cared for at all times.

The Angelic Mothers.

Meditation

Connection of the
Heart to Divine Mother

Beloved Sisters and Brothers of Love and Light, we are the Angelic Mothers coming forth to you now, and we wish to share with you a little more about what a spiritual path is. One's spiritual path is unique and cannot be compared to others'. It may, at times, have similarities, but remember that each one of you has a different vibration, a different experience of incarnations which vibrates in beautiful colours and sounds to us. Therefore, it is imperative that you keep in mind the unique experiences you had on different levels and in different worlds also.

The first step for you to engage on your spiritual path is to make peace with yourself, forgive yourself for what has been. From there you can begin to forgive others and ask for forgiveness, no matter what it was. It all comes to what was missing love in your words, thoughts, and actions.

So today, we wish to accompany you, to open your heart even more, and to engage on your special journey. There will be two steps in this meditation. The first is forgiveness. The second is preparing your heart for your spiritual journey, which will bring you to connect with Divine Mother with more ease and grace for you to receive Her wisdom and guidance in your life.

Begin by taking a few deep breaths once you have grounded your energy and intend for your heart chakra and energy field to expand.

Gently, Angelic Mothers step forth and create a beautiful circle around you. As they take place, they begin to sound to elevate you into a beautiful temple of love and healing where you will receive today, for your highest good, the healings of your heart and your soul so you can embark on your spiritual journey.

Feel yourself into this beautiful temple of love; you are now invited to take place on a crystal table which has a violet flame beneath it and beautiful rose petals of many colours cover the ground around the table. As you lay down on the table, allow yourself to let go of all the tensions in your body, in your mind. Give yourself permission to free yourself from what is holding you back at this point and the permission to allow the clearing and liberation to occur.

The Angelic Mothers assigned to you begin to connect their heart to yours now. This is to assist you in holding the frequency steady and elevated and also to bring more love into your heart for all that lives there and no longer serves you and prevents you from forgiving yourself. All the thought-forms, fears, judgment, belief systems, and patterns are being enveloped into this gentle love.

Some parts of you feel like they do not deserve this forgiveness, and we share to them that it is okay for them to heal now. All is perfect in the Divine Plan. God/Goddess loves each and every one and wishes only the best for all souls, every being.

As the vibration of the heart and the energy field of your body rises higher, it begins to detach from your heart all the energies of hurt, vengeance, despair, sadness, and disbelief. All these energies are now lifted by the love-energy poured into your heart now. As these are lifted, you begin to feel and see yourself as worthy of being loved and being Love. With the energy of Love increasing, you begin to connect to the possibilities of forgiveness and so do other parts of you. These parts of you are invited to come to the temple of Love to receive at the same time as you, which will bring a deeper acknowledgement of your spiritual path and the power of your Divine Love. Continue connecting to your heart and to receive from us, the Angelic Mothers. As we begin now to release all the filaments, the ties that have been put in place long ago by you and by others to bind you in, the belief of not receiving any longer any assistance and holding you into a loop of disempowerment.

Beloved One, we share with you that at this point it is important for you to trust your heart, your divine heart, as it holds many answers and so much wisdom for you. Continue to focus on your heart centre and allow it to expand now as the energies of forgiveness begin to activate within you.

We invite you now to state: *I forgive myself for all actions that lacked love and light. I forgive myself for not allowing myself to be true to myself. I forgive myself for the words that have hurt others. I forgive myself now for_____, I forgive myself for_____, I forgive myself now for_____.*

And I choose to bring love to all of these and to give them over into the violet flame to be transmuted.

I choose now to let the Divine Love flow through my heart so it may expand even more and be filled at all times.

I choose now to embrace the Divine Love in my heart.

Now we invite you to forgive others who have hurt you; intentionally or not; in this lifetime or any other life by stating this: *Through the love of my heart, I forgive you and surrender all of it to my Divine Presence so it can all be cleared for both of us, for all the attachments and ties to be released now. I release all energies that I have been holding back from you and give them over to your Divine Presence so in turn you receive the blessings of this forgiveness.*

And now you are invited to ask for forgiveness to all who have been hurt in any way or shape in this lifetime and other lifetimes through all dimensions. Simply state now: *Through the love of my heart, I ask for all whom I have hurt in this lifetime or other lifetimes to forgive me. I recognize now that some of my actions and words did not come from the Divine Love of my heart, and I am sorry. I choose now to send you only love, for you to receive love on this day in recognition of these connections and for the clearing of all ties, filaments that have held you back and kept you in disempowerment of any sorts. I now ask my Divine Presence to bring you the blessings for your heart. I give thanks now for all the forgiveness I receive this day and embrace the beautiful energies of love that flow freely now through my heart. I give thanks, I give thanks, I give thanks.*

We invite you now to take the time needed with this process and breathe into the love-energy which permeates more deeply your heart centre, chakra.

We begin now connecting to your spiritual body through your heart chakra, filling it with love, wrapping the fears, blockages, and wounds that have prevented you from engaging on your spiritual path. We understand and know all the endeavours your soul has gone through for so many lifetimes, all the tribulations and turmoil it had to surmount as a spiritual being. We are honoured to be of assistance today, to clear some of those fears, blockages, and wounds so you can open your heart and reconnect to your spiritual body through the love-energy and begin to walk on your spiritual path again in full consciousness and to feel free to be the spiritual being that you are.

Take some more deep breaths now and give permission for all that is blocking you from walking your spiritual path to be released. Do you give us permission to act in your name to clear these blocks?

Thank you, Dear One.

We say to you, Dear One, one lifetime has brought some closure in your spiritual body, shutting it down to a point where you could not be noticed by anyone close or far from you; you were even undetected. We know so many souls have gone through this, trying to protect themselves, and we share with you these times are over for you. You can now release all the wounds, fears, blocks, beliefs, thought-forms, and patterns that have kept you from embracing your divine spiritual path in this life.

We now begin to gently release the attachments that have kept you disconnected from your spiritual path, clearing now all obstacles preventing you from moving forward on your spiritual path, clearing all energies that no longer serve you, and supporting your spiritual body for your highest good.

We begin to pour forth elixirs of love into your heart chakra and your spiritual body now, which will calibrate the energy of each one of them, assist them to raise the frequency and to realign them with your divine plan and with your entire bodily system.

We begin to sing now to bring more ease and grace into this process. You now begin to receive the frequency of this chant, which strengthens your heart energy and the energy of your spiritual body now. Continue breathing and receiving these energies for a moment now whilst we care for all the parts of you that have come forth to receive with you. They thank you for inviting them as they now are healed and return to the light. Your Divine Presence blesses all of you now.

You are now invited to take the **Code: *Connection of the Heart to Divine Mother*** that has been prepared for you to connect with the Divine Mother. Look into this Code and allow it to enter your brow chakra and go down gently all the way into your heart where you will receive the connection to the Divine Mother's heart. Breathe deeply as you look into it, and once you feel it into your heart, begin to sing the mantra thirty-three times (33X) whilst looking into the Code.

This Code will clear fears of connecting to the Divine Mother and assist in opening your heart to receive more love. This will assist you on your spiritual path; you will connect to Her heart and be able to receive Her love and support when needed beloved.

Now that you are done with the Code, we the Angelic Mothers begin singing to bring you back into your sacred space.

We invite you to hydrate yourself and walk in nature to fully ground what you have received today.

We give thanks for all that has been healed, forgiven, and embraced this day.

Blessed be, Blessed be, Blessed be all who walk the path of love.

We are the Angelic Mothers.

Namaste.

CONNECTION OF THE HEART TO DIVINE MOTHER

Nicole Kishalah 2020

A MI NA ME KARI A TO AMI NA ME (33X)

Conclusion

Embarking on your personal journey *Back to Love* means you have a lot of courage, compassion, and love for yourself. It is a path of discovery and is a beautiful journey, one that is worth it to start at any age, at any time in your life. You now have tools to assist you to come back to your heart again.

Once you have done the meditations and activated the Codes, you can use any of these when needed as you have already activated them. They will bring you the support you need in that moment.

I wish you all the best on your journey back to love, back to your heart's essence, which is Love.

Love and blessings,
Nicole Thibodeau

Acknowledgments

Thank you to all who before me channeled and paved the way for me so I could open my heart and heal with more ease and grace. Thank you for your courage and determination.

My teachers, mentors, and friends who have held me and encouraged me through my journey.

My family of light, always by my side holding me and encouraging me to go beyond my beliefs and imagination.

I was graced with four amazing children. Thank you for believing in my message and encouraging me to keep going and being some of my teachers.

And to my wonderful husband who supports me in all my endeavours, through thick and thin, and always has faith in me and my message. Your love means the world to me. Love you!

About the Author

Nicole Thibodeau is an Oracle of Divine Transmissions. As a Channeler and Mentor, she is like the conduit or wire that connects to you and to Source through which Divine Guidance flows. When she channels, it is like being wrapped in, held, and cocooned in a safe, warm blanket of motherly love and light. But what she is most passionate about is assisting people to embrace their Divine Power and be the master of their life.

She always has been a strong believer in God and the Angels. In fact, they were her best friends, and she always spoke to them as her equals. She is highly intuitive and was about five years old when she received her first Angelic message. She channels various Beings of Light, the Divine Mother, and the Angelic Mothers.

In 2007, after experiencing a near-death situation following a surgery, it became clear to her that she was being called to pursue her spiritual destiny as a healer and channeler.

When she works she uses light language and Toning for:

- Its power of Sound
- To elevate the frequencies
- To activate, clear, and align the chakras and anchor energies

She also creates Codes, which are channeled images infused with high frequencies, to assist her clients to activate energies in a very simple, gentle, and yet powerful way. For more than a decade now, she has been working as a channeler. She has brought through her teachings, healings, Codes, and paintings, and in recent years, it has led her to mentoring people and groups through the different programs she has developed.

She is a Certified Quest for Mastery teacher, a graduate from the Gaïa Mystery School, Open to Channel course, Self-Mastery School of Loving Presence and also is a Reiki Master. Recently, she began working as a speaker and is an author.

Connect with Nicole

Connect with me to know more about
my activities and mentoring.

Website: www.nicolethibodeau.ca
E-mail address: info@nicolethibodeau.ca
Facebook: @nicolethibodeau.ca
Instagram: @nicolethibodeau.ca

*If you wish to print out the
codes for your personal use, use this link:*
https://bit.ly/BTLACodes

You will receive an email with instructions
to access a PDF of all the codes.

Read more by Nicole in:

Navigating the Clickety Clack: How to Live a Peace-filled Life in a Seemingly Toxic World (Volume 3) is an international bestselling book in which co-authors share their experience of how they are able to stay peaceful inside, no matter what is happening outside and in time of changes.

Manufactured by Amazon.ca
Bolton, ON